The Nine Scoundrels

How to Recognize and Release Subtle Patterns of Sabotage

Deanna Reiter

This book is available at special quantity discounts for bulk purchases for sales promotions, premiums or fund raising. Special books or book excerpts can also be created to fit specific needs. For details, please contact the author through her website: www.dayawati.com.

The information in this book is not designed to replace medical advice and is used at the reader's discretion.

Text design and typography by Joel Van Valin.

FIRST PRINTING 2008

ISBN: 978-0-98003755-5

Joy

It lingers —
   Dancing
   Summoning
   Awaiting us
To open the gateway
And let it in.

They sit —
   Quietly
   Ever present
   Omnipotent
   Wanting us
To accept them
As ourselves.

They are here
And now
      Ready to grasp
      And savor
The most blissful state
We desire to reside
      Stealing our claim
      Owning our power
      Believing that they can
Have all the happiness
Of which we dream.

But the reality is —

It is we
      Who have all the power
      That we choose to accept

It is we
      Who own all the bliss
      That we choose to create

It is we
      Who must believe that we
      Can live everyday
In Ultimate Joy.

                    - DR   23 May 2007

Table of Contents

I would like to acknowledge every living being in thought and form and Baba and Hana — relentless and unyielding.

May you, dear reader, live in a continuous state of peace and joy on a journey filled with Truth, Simplicity and Love.

Om Namaha Shivaya

Introduction

At the end of my first book, *Dancing with Divinity: Positive Affirmations for any Situation*, I announced that my next book, entitled *Ultimate Joy*, would be released in 2008. When *Ultimate Joy* was near completion, I discovered that *The Nine Scoundrels* were stealing the show and I changed the book's name. The title of the book changed, but the focal point remains the same: How to live your life in ultimate joy.

In the early stages of the first draft, back when it was still called *Ultimate Joy*, I had my manuscript in hand aboard a plane. Two young boys seated behind me broke into a lively rendition of "If You're Happy and You Know it Clap Your Hands." Already joyful, I smiled at the brothers.

I thought about the synchronicity of hearing the song as I was paging through notes for the book. I thought about the lack of inhibition the boys had in expressing their excitement about the plane ride. I remembered how fun it was to be a kid, full of anticipation and joy, able to live in total bliss knowing that all your needs were met and you were safe and protected. I thought about how great it is that kids have the willingness to express this joy without worrying what anyone thought.

And I wondered how many people on the plane were as happy as those boys at that moment. There were probably a handful of people that were indifferent to the two singing brothers, a few annoyed people and perhaps only a handful as happy as the young boys. Since this was a six o'clock Monday morning flight to Detroit, it's likely most people would rather have been somewhere else.

The song reaffirmed to me the need to find happiness in the most humdrum, routine activities in our lives. It also reminded me of the need to find the joy that allows us to wake up refreshed, excited and energetic about the day ahead. The joy we can have knowing there is nothing we would rather be doing than what we are doing right now. The joy that we find when we overcome difficult moments through courage and confidence. The joy within sorrow and loss. The joy that we express when we are present in the world with smiles on our faces.

It is this joy that we can have every moment of every day. We need only to access it.

However, there can be people, situations and little "scoundrels" that attempt to get in the way of our joy. None of them are necessarily bad or wrong. It is simply a matter of how we perceive them. If we approach everything as a new adventure or opportunity for growth and experience, we can meet any challenge that presents itself.

So, how do we get back to the simple bliss of childhood? How do we free ourselves of the scoundrels that are present in our lives? How do we remain in a state of ultimate joy?

A big key to living in ultimate joy is to recognize and release the nine dominant roles that humans play. Any of these roles could be present within us without our awareness, similar to a hidden parasite; therefore they are referred to in this book as scoundrels. Scoundrels can be lurking within us at different times in our lives, perhaps dormant for years until you meet someone who has a similar scoundrel that awakens yours. Sometimes, these scoundrels may or may not be recognized by us, but a friend or family member might see them within us. Although the idea of little scoundrels stealing your joy is meant playfully, this book has a serious purpose. It is important to take ownership of your scoundrel and your thoughts, emotions and actions that keep you from living joyfully. Do not view yourself as a victim controlled by scoundrels. Do not ignore the reality that you and the scoundrel are one and the same.

Look at The Nine Scoundrels Chart on pages 20-21. It offers dialogue for each of the scoundrels. Detailed descriptions of each scoundrel can be found in the following chapters. Read about them with unbiased objectivity, as though you are from another planet observing the human race. Do not assign scoundrels to yourself or anyone you know.

After you have an understanding of each role, ask yourself how you might fit into that category. Verify that the description of the scoundrel(s) you have chosen is indeed the most similar to patterns that you have acted out in your life. Whether you recognize patterns of being stuck in the past or addicted to misery in yourself or others, do not judge or blame yourself or anyone else for having these patterns.

Examine the similarities between yourself and the scoundrels. Remember the last time you acted like any of them. After each category, read and answer the questions to better examine your motive for being like that scoundrel. Complete any exercises suggested. Read the affirmations to release the scoundrel mentality you have incorporated into your life. You can also write them, paint them, shout them and walk with them. Record them and listen to them during the day or when you're falling asleep at night. Try any and all methods to move into a new way of thinking and move out of your former mind-set.

The entire process that you will undertake is called the **Observe – Verify – Examine – Release Technique, or the OVER Technique**. This technique can be used for any habit, thought, pattern or action that you want to change in your life. By first observing it, you can then verify why you believe the thought arose or the action occurred. You can then examine the reasons or motivations behind the thought or action and then release it and replace it with what is more beneficial for you. With this technique, you can see to it that you are finished with what had not been working in your life. Essentially, your relationship with that particular scoundrel is **OVER**.

You may notice that you have patterns similar to a few scoundrels. You may be able to identify with all nine of them. Rather than getting overwhelmed and defeated by this recognition, simply read through them one at a time. You could spend one week or one year moving through the **OVER Technique** for one scoundrel before moving on to another. You can pick one scoundrel from the chart and skip ahead to the chapter on that scoundrel. You could read through the entire book and then return to whichever chapter you choose. The subchapters for each scoundrel provide further suggestions for moving forward. Allow yourself total freedom while reading these sections. Incorporate the ideas in your own way and at your own pace. Now is your opportunity to take control of the little scoundrels lurking in you.

Checking in

Close your eyes and take a deep breath. Release it. Allow your shoulders to relax, your tongue to drop from the roof of your mouth and your jaw to become slack. Check in with yourself. How are you doing right now? If you answered that you are cold, put on a sweater, grab a blanket or exercise for ten minutes. If you're tired, close your eyes and rest. If you're anxious or worried about something, take a few minutes to journal and release your anxiety on paper or take a few deep breaths and release your worry to the Universe. If you answered with anything less than, "I'm doing great," figure out what it is that you need and take care of yourself. If you are operating at less than your ideal, you are serving no one as effectively as you could be.

Unfortunately, this is where many of us *are* operating. We are running around like monkeys, not content and not clear why we lack contentment.

But if we are doing great, then our lives have to be perfect, right?

And since perfection seems impossible then contentment must be impossible, too, you might think. But simply by staying in the present moment, we find that our lives are perfect and happy right this very second. Even if you just got a horrible hair cut or your car has a flat tire or your child got suspended from school, your life can be perfect. If you embrace the current moment, you can find contentment.

Again, close your eyes and take a deep breath. Take another. And another. And for two or ten or twenty minutes or even a full hour, allow yourself to relax and to take an opportunity to check in with yourself. Spend time with yourself.

As humans, we tend to avoid the present as much as we can. We think about the future and the past. We attempt to do ten different things at once to distract us from the present moment.

Do we distract ourselves because our lives are not perfect?

Or have we been taught to believe that our lives are not perfect? Have we been taught to see what is missing in our lives rather than to recognize and be grateful for what we have?

We may have been taught that we, as human beings, are not good enough. We are guilty. We are sinners. We are naughty children. We are greedy. We have ruined the planet. We are out of balance. These messages have been passed down from one generation to the next. Our parents, our grandparents, ministers and anyone whom we have put in a position of authority have shared these messages. Our imperfections have been thrown at us. These false messages have been filtered into our psyche. They result in keeping many of the scoundrels present in our lives. They have helped solidify the belief that we are not perfect. Because we lack perfection, we therefore cannot be content.

The advertising industry adds to this message of imperfection. Products appeal to the masses by telling us how we can be thinner, better looking, smell great, have healthier skin and hair, and so on. Most Westerners have healthy, white teeth, but if there's an advertisement telling us about a product to make our teeth even whiter, we want the product. Whiter teeth certainly will bring us more happiness, right? The ad subliminally suggests that we wouldn't be happy if we didn't have porcelain-white teeth like the model in the commercial. Without their product, we are lacking the whitest teeth possible and therefore we are imperfect. Lack of status, lack of happiness, lack of beauty – you name it; ads constantly bombard us with newer and better products to make us slimmer, healthier, richer, better looking, smarter, bustier and younger. The messages being conveyed are:

You are not good enough.
You do not have enough.
You do not do enough.
You will be happier when...
You would be happier if only...

How often do we take in these messages? We hear them on the radio, watch them on television and read them in newspapers and magazines. We see them on billboards, bus stops and park benches. The list is virtually limitless. The bigger the city, the more the ad industry preys.

Even when we don't pay much attention to these ads, the subliminal, subconscious effect is apparent. Our brain becomes aware of the ads on some level. And if the product is slightly practical, the message lingers: *I could use that. My life would be better if I had that.*

The messages are a subtle and consistent reminder that we are living with a scarcity mentality. Many of them leave us feeling competitive or jealous, dwelling on our self-proclaimed imperfections. They leave us feeling unhappy.

We become programmed in lacking perfection. We then lack self-confidence. This means that in at least one area of our lives we feel inferior. Perhaps we have confidence at work and in sports, but we lack confidence with the opposite sex or in public speaking.

Whatever we lack confidence in, reflects the areas of our lives where we are not happy and where we are harboring negative thoughts. When we can change our thoughts and our perception, our situation usually changes. Thinking positively and using positive affirmations can boost our confidence and harness better situations around us. Looking to past successes in the areas in which we have struggled reaffirms that we can succeed in these areas again, if only we believe that we can.

We also remain unsatisfied and unhappy because of fear. We are scared that if we communicate our needs directly – to our co-workers, our boss, our neighbors – we will be rejected. We may believe we'll be left in a worse situation. In reality, however, this is seldom the case. The good of human nature responds to meet the needs of others. Even if we are rejected and left in a "worse" situation, it is only perceived as worse by us in the present moment. It opens us for something better to enter our lives.

We have a fear of happiness. What would happen if everything in our lives shifted and we found contentment? Many of us have the beliefs: *Life is hard. Life is not fair. There is never enough time or money. You can never be too rich or too thin.* We make these statements without even realizing what we are saying.

Take some time and get everything working perfectly in one area of your life. Make it something very significant, like contentment in your job, your home, in your relationships or your health. See how long it is before you can find something wrong again. Because we are taught that life is hard and unfair, we find ways to create this for ourselves. We may finally complete every project in our home and have it decorated and organized perfectly. How long can we stay living in this state? Many times, when people have everything exactly as they want it, they move.

The same can be seen in other areas of our existence. If we can't handle perfection, we manifest a problem. Imagine getting a new bicycle or automobile. For some of us, the perfection may be too great. We know that sooner or later we'll get our vehicle dirty or it will somehow get a scratch. We might actually take a key and put a tiny scratch into the paint to make it imperfect. This way, when it does get an unplanned scratch, we won't be as upset.

This also holds true in relationships. When relationships seem too perfect, we need to create conflict to make them seem more "normal." After all, if we don't love ourselves, how can we be in relationships with people who love us so much? There must be something wrong with *them*, we rationalize, because we know there's something wrong with *us*.

We can also create problems based on our unconscious beliefs in our jobs. We may have a conscious or unconscious thought that work isn't fun; work is hard; the only type of work that is rewarding is the type that really challenges us; we need to work hard in order to play hard. We end up being unhappy in our careers because of these negative, false beliefs. Why not have rewarding careers that are fun and effortless? Doesn't it make sense for everyone to get paid doing what they *love*?

We are not here to struggle in our jobs or to focus on a paycheck. We are not here to be unhappy, spewing our complaints and our ingratitude at every opportunity. We are not here to see how many classes we can take and errands we can accomplish. We are not here to be in a constant state of doing, moving so quickly on autopilot that we cannot remember one day from the next.

We linger with unhappiness because we are addicted to the reality we have created. Sure, we don't *like* the fact that our marriage isn't working, but it seems simpler to complain about it to our friends who are also miserable, than to communicate directly to our spouses. It also seems simpler to be miserable than to dig deep within ourselves and recognize and change what is not ideal in our lives.

We become addicted to our dramas, our misery and our unhappiness. It doesn't matter if it's our marriages, our careers, our friendships, our lack of time, money, love or health. We find an unhealthy comfort in staying with what is not working rather than step into the unknown or deal with the problem at hand. We refuse to part with our dramas and our misery just as children remain attached to their tattered and torn baby blankets. The most phenomenal person or circumstance could be just around the corner, but we never make that turn. We never let go of our familiar agony to discover unfamiliar bliss.

We also tend to delay our happiness as long as we possibly can. Sometimes we are only moved to action when it is for someone else. We put other people's happiness ahead of our own. Indirectly, we will gain happiness from this. But how about taking responsibility for our own happiness? Why not summon the people and circumstances that we need in order to be content?

Isn't that selfish?

It ceases to be seen as selfish when we become aware that if we are unhappy in a situation, we carry that unhappiness to everyone with whom we come in contact. We become carriers of gloom and detract from people's lives rather than add to their lives. With that understanding, we see how it is our duty to be happy and to add our joyful energy to the world.

Another simple thing we fail to do is *strive* for contentment. We become complacent and indifferent. When asked to rate something on a scale of one to ten, most people will shy away from extremes. People will typically aim for the middle ground. They are likely to choose a number between four and seven. Say for example, they're rating their career and they give it a six. Why a six? No reason in particular, they answer, everything's fine, but it could always be better, right?

The messages we have collected from our families, our religions, our society and advertising have combined within our collective unconscious. These messages have become our beliefs, whether we are aware of them or not. We have taken these messages and manifested them into scoundrels that keep us from living in ultimate joy.

Each of these scoundrels has a unique way of sabotaging our happiness. But again, it is our perception and our individual thoughts and actions that can get in our way in the presence of these scoundrels. We have invented and invited the scoundrels into our lives. It is simple and easy to release them, however. We need only become aware of them in order to be free.

Many of us believe that things could always be better. Living in ultimate joy requires that we strive for contentment *as it stands now.*

This doesn't mean we should be complacent and settle for what is less than ideal. It means we can be active in seeking contentment. It means that we move away from complaint and misery. It means that it's time for us to determine what we need to be content and to manifest it. And along the way, no matter what stage we are at, we can be grateful for all that we have been given and all that is being prepared for us. There are many forces working together for our happiness.

Now that you are conscious of the possibility for continual joy, make it your reality.

The Nine Scoundrels Chart

"This broken window doesn't let in much rain."

"Only six more years until..."

"If you think that's bad, listen to this..."

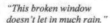

Complacent
(thinks things are good enough)

Delayed Gratification
(waits for what might make them happy)

Addicted to Misery
(enjoys complaining)

"I'd better skip that free trip to the amusement park."

"I can't go to the beach, I have to cut my neighbor's grass."

Fear of Happiness
(thinks too much pleasure will result in something bad)

Martyr
(puts other people's joy before their own)

Negative Thinking
(assumes the worst)

"I don't think they'll hire me."

Stuck in the Past
(remembers past wrongs & mistakes)

"If only I had done that a little differently."

Forward Thinking
(lives with a sense of anxiety & urgency)

"After I clean the house, I'll get groceries and then I'll..."

Grass is Greener
(believes happiness lies outside of themselves)

"I want the same jacket Sam has."

I
Complacent Scoundrel

Complacent Scoundrels have determined that life is okay as it is, even though it is far from ideal. They believe life is not perfect, but nothing is perfect, therefore it is good enough. They think life is unfair. They believe they must learn to live with the cards they were dealt rather than trade in any of their old cards. After all, the Complacent Scoundrels rationalize, they might end up with new cards that are even worse. These Scoundrels are unmotivated to change what is making them unhappy. Fear of the unknown is a major factor in their lack of motivation.

Perhaps they are not willing or able to identify the sources of their unhappiness. Or they may not recognize that they are unhappy. Repressed sadness or depression occurs in Complacent Scoundrels. Long-term stress can physically manifest itself as a chronic disease.

Complacent Scoundrels also do not want to rustle anyone's feathers. They do not want anyone to make a big fuss over them, even if it truly would bring them more happiness. When others act on their behalf, it sheds light on their lack of motivation to change.

Complacent Scoundrels tend to be frugal and conservative in their spending habits to the point of ridiculousness, where their penny-pinching becomes a detriment to them and to those close to them. They might drive out of their way for a "deal," not considering the cost of gas and the time they waste. On a positive note, they are typically hard workers and are extremely loyal in areas regarding work, family, friends and religion.

There may be relationships that are sub par, living or job situations that are not ideal and unhealthy lifestyle choices that seem

23

impossible to change. The perceived consequences of altering what is not working in their lives seem insurmountable. They believe it will be too difficult to fight the current beliefs, patterns, values or prejudices of their family, religion or culture. Lack of motivation and fear of the unknown keep them stuck, refusing to examine their unhappiness or the causes of it.

Happiness comes to the Complacent Scoundrels through this unconscious filter. They tend to choose the second best or opt away from their first choice because they have become conditioned to accept what is "good enough," perhaps believing that the "top of the line" item is "over the top" and unnecessary. They are highly unlikely to be trendsetters or technologically crazed. They have brainwashed themselves into believing that other people's second choice is the best choice for them and that people must be blind not to see this.

Complacent Scoundrels seem easy going, laid back and indifferent. Many appear to be happy from the outside. They have "settled," but they may not recognize this within themselves. A deeply rooted feeling of dissatisfaction pervades inside them and may only be recognized in major components of their life, such as not being fulfilled in their career or marriage. In reality, if they were to dig deeper, they would discover that their complacency and tendency to settle has affected many other facets of their lives.

It is important that Complacent Scoundrels recognize their past patterns of complacency so that they live happier and more fulfilled lives. Everything that is sub par can become ideal for them as they realize their true self-worth and their individual preferences and take action to manifest them.

Typically, an external motivator prods Complacent Scoundrels into action. They often do not shake things up on their own accord; rather they are pushed to make a change. For instance, they might not leave bad marriages; their spouses leave instead. They might not leave a bad job unless they are fired or laid off. Someone in their lives might first be an example to them and then Complacent Scoundrels follow the lead. Without some impetus to change, Complacent Scoundrels are seemingly content and willing to make do with a less than ideal status quo.

Comments you might hear from Complacent Scoundrels:

"I can make do with that."
"Well, sure it could be better, but…"
"It's good enough."
"Don't bother if it's too much trouble."
"It's been this way for years and I've learned to live with it just fine."
"If it ain't broke, don't fix it."
"I can't quit. What if I never find another job?"

If you OBSERVE and VERIFY the Complacent Scoundrel in your life, EXAMINE the following:

1. How has the Complacent Scoundrel helped you?
2. How has it negatively affected you?
3. To the best of your recollection, when were you first introduced to the Complacent Scoundrel? Is this a family, cultural or societal scoundrel you consciously or unconsciously accepted as your own?
4. What are some examples of how you've been a Complacent Scoundrel in the past week?
5. On a scale of one to ten, ten being the best, how would you rate your overall level of satisfaction and happiness in life?
6. What situations, people or things have you settled for in your life that have left you with less than ideal situations?
7. How can you make your life more ideal? What is one thing you can do TODAY to reinvent your life by releasing what is not serving your highest good?

RELEASE the Complacent Scoundrel Mentality with the following Affirmations:

ॐ *I create my reality.*
ॐ *I deserve to be happy.*
ॐ *I deserve a perfect job.*
ॐ *I deserve a perfect place to live.*
ॐ *I deserve respect.*

ॐ *Only loving, peaceful people deserve to be in my life.*

ॐ *Everyone in my world wants what is best for me.*

ॐ *The Universe supports my happiness.*

ॐ *I now choose to be in perfect situations.*

ॐ *I deserve the best that life has to offer me.*

ॐ *I choose to live a life of excitement and awe.*

ॐ *I deserve an ideal relationship with myself and others.*

ॐ *I am generous with myself and others.*

ॐ *I choose to exercise and eat well for my health.*

Conscious, Independent Thought

Nearly everyone is affected by other people's thoughts and feelings. Our emotional energy can be affected by our surroundings. For example, in a group meeting, someone who fidgets and often checks his watch makes other people feel anxious. If we become susceptible to this anxiety, when it is our turn to lead the group, we may speed through our section. Although we are not in a hurry ourselves, we feel the need to rush.

We learn from an early age what is acceptable in our culture and what is not, regardless of what is acceptable for us individually. Although our egos like to believe that we have unique and ingenious thoughts, most of us think the same thought patterns each day, which are recycled in our society at large. The unconscious thought in the world accumulated from present and past generations is the collective unconscious, or *spiritus mundi* (Latin for "world spirit"), which encompasses the beliefs and ethics of a society.

Take a look at how you stay within the safe parameters of your society. What are some societal views that you uphold but that don't really apply to you? Do you believe in having grass in your yard? Do you believe in a religion? Do you believe in matching your clothes? Do you believe in wearing jewelry? Do you believe in sleeping in a bed? Do you believe in sleeping at night and being awake during the day? Do you believe in eating with a spoon or fork? Do you dress up in a weird costume only on October 31?

Have you ever examined why you do these things or have you simply chosen to do them because that is what you've been taught or because that is what everyone else does? Have you grown complacent in your thinking and become complacent in your actions?

Have you ever thought about tearing up all the grass in your yard and having a rock garden, wildflowers or a vegetable garden? Have you ever challenged the beliefs of your religion or experienced all the major world religions? Have you tried mismatching your clothes to be different and to experience people's reactions? Have you ever gone without any jewelry for a long period of time or questioned why anyone wears it? Have you tried sleeping on a mat or on the floor for several months or years to see if you like it? Have you experimented with every possible sleeping pattern to figure out what works best for you? Have you used chopsticks or bread or your fingers to scoop up your food rather than silverware? Do you dress up in a unique way whenever you want?

Just as there is no single diet that is going to work well for every human being, there is no single best plant for every yard, single best religion or single best sleeping arrangement. It is up to you to choose what works best for you. You may decide to paint purple hearts on your house, never leave your home without donning your pterodactyl hat and consume three limes each day to stave off cataracts. Do what seems natural and right for *you*. This will get you thinking outside the box and get others to expand their thinking as well. It will also allow people to be themselves without fear of disapproval.

The benefit to breaking out of dogmatic thought is that new ideas get generated. Better ways of doing things are discovered. Creativity flourishes. People become more open-minded and liberated. They release their complacency and a higher level of constructive thinking occurs. A deeper level of comprehension is developed through experience.

The more we can live within a construct that works best for us and is unique to us, the higher our quality of life will be. When we fail to question the collective beliefs and ways of society, we become complacent because we rely on other people's experiences rather than have our own experience. This is not entirely bad. We can trust the negative experience of heroine addicts rather than have our own bad experience with heroine. But realize that having a herd mentality can also harm you.

For instance, it can influence your longevity. Let's say you discover that the average life span for the Western world is approximately seventy years old. You will absorb that knowledge on some level and believe that you will live to be about seventy years old (unless you had family members that have lived beyond seventy to serve as examples to you). If the average life span increased to one hundred, you would open your mind to the possibility of living to one hundred. With modern technology, safe drinking water and conscious, independent thought, we may have the potential to live much longer than this. When we see this demonstrated more often as the norm within society, we will believe it enough to see an increase in longevity. But it's unnecessary and impractical to wait to see this improvement. It makes far more sense to test the hypothesis yourself.

Engaging in conscious, independent thought also allows you to see alternatives within the areas of medicine, transportation, energy, education, business, government, economics, science and theology. Instead of believing what you have been told, experience it as true for *you*. Perhaps you look into Chinese and holistic medicine as well as Western medicine for remedies to an illness. Perhaps you realize that an alternative education program is more ideal than a public education for a particular child. Perhaps you envision how an alternative money system can be more effective in your community than the currency currently used.

Things become improved when we critically think and move beyond current methods. It may seem fine to sweep your floor with a two-foot tall broom, but what if you try a broom with a five-foot tall handle? Does your back feel better after sweeping with a taller broom? Then use the taller broom. If you prefer the shorter broom, then use that one. Make adjustments to all thoughts, ideas and concepts just like this. Test what needs testing. Trust in what you know is intuitively right for you. Move into a higher state of awareness and consciousness in all you think, say and do. The more conscious we become, the more we gain control of our thoughts and emotions. As this occurs, we function at a significantly higher level, gaining mastery of our lives.

Power

Humans are born with an ability to command power. In the womb, we are the ultimate power parasite, having all of our needs met and everyone expectant to meet us (See Chapter Three: Addicted to Misery Scoundrel: Recognize That You Create Your Reality). As babies, we are nurtured and protected. We beckon help with a mere cry. Throughout childhood and adolescence, this power begins to wane, although we think we are becoming more powerful because we are getting bigger and growing stronger. We begin to take on more duties and responsibilities, but we no longer harness the reverence we did at the beginning of our physical existence.

When we reach adulthood, we gain more power than we did as children by gaining our freedom and independence. We move into the world and fend for ourselves. We have power of choice, thoughts, words and actions. We have financial power and voting power. We gain greater power through the machines we use and the networks we establish. But in many aspects of our lives, we feel powerless.

Maybe we feel we do not get the respect or recognition we deserve. Maybe there are certain people in our lives that refuse to listen to us, no matter what we are saying or how much it would benefit them. Maybe we feel subordinate at work or in a relationship. These situations that we have attracted keep us weak and agitated because we know what it once was to have ultimate power. It is easy for Complacent Scoundrels to thrive when a discrepancy exists between our ideal and our reality.

Power can be increased in four simple ways:

- honor yourself
- honor your passion
- honor your neighbor
- honor your higher power

There are plenty of self-empowerment tools in the world. Your mind is the very best of these tools. Conscious, positive thought will give you the groundwork for self-empowerment. Your belief in these thoughts will solidify the foundation. Your words and actions are the final ingredients. You honor yourself through your thought, belief and manifestation. Your self-respect becomes evident when you are living a life of joy and peace one hundred percent of the time, in all aspects of your life. If you are currently at a place where your self-respect is low and a great deal of work needs to be done in order to move you into a place of self-respect and self-love, embrace the challenge. Begin by observing ways in which you are not honoring yourself. Recognize when you do not eat healthy foods or when you are deprived of sleep. Examine why you are doing this. Next time you find yourself in the same situation, release the pattern of abuse you have formerly established and honor yourself with conscious choices.

Honoring your passion is also an important key to reclaiming your power. Discover the things that make you feel alive and vibrant. Do them as often as possible. Feel the power, confidence and joy that you gain through your passion.

Honoring your friend or neighbor is another way to retrieve power. This may seem like backward thinking because we have learned that we gain power when we have power *over* someone. Instead, your power increases by honoring everyone you meet and giving them your full attention. Consider your "neighbor" to be all things outside of yourself – the elements, the plants, the animals, all humans and all animate and inanimate objects. Increase the joy in their lives. Treat them with respect.

"Lisa" was considering leaving her job as a furniture salesperson. Disappointed that the job no longer met her needs and that she would have to look elsewhere for employment, she decided she would give up all expectations she had of her job, including her commission. Instead, she would focus on the customers with genuine sincerity. With that adjustment, she had her biggest week of sales and soon became the leading salesperson in the district.

Trust your instincts to avoid certain people and leave situations that do not support your highest good. Put your energy into people and situations that feel right. Keep a pure motive behind everything that you do.

Honoring your higher power is the ultimate way to harness the infinite power of the Universe. Spend time each day in meditation and stillness, so that you can listen to and connect with your higher power. (Read Chapter Five: Martyr Scoundrel: Find a Higher Connection.)

Your power will naturally develop when you cultivate honor in these four ways.

Do Something Nice

Make a difference in someone else's life to rid the Complacent Scoundrel mentality. By doing something nice for someone else, you will be more open to accept help from other people.

Perhaps your career is one in which you are serving other people. This allows you to do nice things for people throughout your day. You can gain a great sense of fulfillment from this. Perhaps you have many opportunities to help your friends and family throughout the day as well. Maybe you take care of your children or an ailing parent. Maybe you are helping a friend with a crisis. These are wonderful examples of serving others.

For the next few days or weeks, step beyond the realm of your job or any commitments you make to your friends and family. Do something generous for a complete stranger. Make it something fairly big, beyond a compliment or holding the door for them. Offer to watch your neighbors' children for an hour or two so they can do an errand. Give clothes to charity. Volunteer at a school or nursing home. Give blood. Bring food to a homeless person. Offer your professional services to someone for free.

By doing something nice for someone, you will know that you are making a difference in the world. Follow your instincts when you have the opportunity to help others. The less you allow others the opportunity to be complacent with what is not working in their lives, the easier it will be to see your own complacency and change it.

Be Generous

"Helen" found herself thousands of dollars in credit card debt. She paid finance charges on her debt every month and simply accepted the predicament she was in, vowing to pay off this debt as soon as she could.

An acquaintance of Helen's discovered the debt and offered to pay it. He wanted to do a good deed without expectation of any type of payback. Apprehensive to accept the thousands of dollars he was offering, she ultimately recognized the gift as coming from the Universe and accepted it. She had always been a generous person and after having received the gift of money, she became even more generous. It is amazing to see how generosity is much like a smile or a positive word of encouragement. As we accept generosity, we desire to pass it onward to another in whatever kind way we can.

The opposite of this is being stingy with ourselves and being stingy with others who then become stingy with us. That is a cycle that is often seen in Complacent Scoundrels. (If you are a Complacent Scoundrel who is generous with other people, but not with yourself, read Chapter Five: Martyr Scoundrel.) This type of limiting behavior can manifest itself in many forms. Money tends to be a very obvious way people can be generous or frugal. But it is also possible to be selfish with your time, in volunteering to help others. You can be stingy with your talents, with lending, sharing or giving away your belongings, with offering your advice, with random acts of kindness, with love and with expressing your emotions.

If we cannot allow ourselves to indulge in a beautiful home-cooked dinner or a night dining out, we will be less likely to offer it to others. If we do not treat ourselves to fresh flowers, we may never deem it necessary to buy flowers for other people. If we never take time out of our busy schedules to enjoy a nice weekend away, we will very likely resent others who enjoy a vacation and we may not offer them any assistance so that their travel plans go smoothly.

By becoming more generous with ourselves, we experience the goodness and richness that life has to offer. When goodness comes to us, it is easier for us to spread that goodness to others. We reflect back to the world what the world gives to us. And the world reflects back to us what we give to the world.

What can you give to yourself that you have not been allowing yourself? What can you give to others that you typically don't?

Challenge yourself in both directions.

The universal karmic law returns to you what you give. If you withhold from yourself or others you are essentially withholding from the Universe. You are also limiting the potential you have within yourself. You are limiting your possibilities. You are limiting your world.

Increase your generosity in ways that you have been limiting. As you give to yourself and others, make sure you are doing so full of joy. If it would make you happy to give away one hundred dollars to a stranger on the street, then give away one hundred dollars. If it would make you miserable, then don't do it. There is no joy found in bitterness and regret. Check in with yourself and do what feels right.

Pull the Plug

A typical Complacent Scoundrel spends a great deal of time in front of the television. (If you happen to be a Complacent Scoundrel who does not watch television, continue on to the next section.) The time spent passively watching television replaces the opportunity for people to interact without the television as mediator. It replaces time that can be spent outdoors with the elements. It steals away time from creative pursuits, such as reading, writing and painting.

A few television shows are emotionally uplifting and convey a good message, but overall television is not fulfilling. Watching someone rape, hit or kill another person does not enhance our emotional state. Violence on television, even if it's make-believe, can desensitize us and precipitate anger. Is it entertaining? Perhaps. Is it emotionally, physically and mentally beneficial? Rarely.

Many news programs promote fear. Headlines often warn us about a bombing, a shooting, a robbery, a storm, an economic crisis, an environmental disaster, a medical epidemic, an international rivalry or something equally destructive. Once in a while, there will be a happy headline, most likely sports-related.

Advertisements create the belief of lack because we conclude that we are not good enough without the advertised products. This keeps us in a perceived state of imperfection, a sure way to fuel Complacent Scoundrels.

The endless stimuli of sight and sound serve as a constant distraction from being alone with ourselves or with others, removing the opportunity for deep, meaningful dialogue. The constant background noise diverts us from the chance for introspection and the opportunity to get in touch with our feelings and true selves. Spending hours watching television diverts time away from areas in our lives that need our energy and attention, helping us to remain complacent.

Spending hours viewing violence, drama and commercial pitches is not healthy. It does not teach us that we are divine creatures and that we are good enough as we are right now. It does not develop our self-esteem and enhance the joy in our lives.

Shut off the television for a period of three nights to three months. If you do not have control of the television viewing in your household, remove yourself from the room. If you're sharing a studio apartment or dorm room and cannot escape the television, go to a sitting room in your building, go outside, visit the library frequently or get ear plugs. Spend your time away from the television doing something you enjoy but have not done for a while.

During your television abstinence, do you notice any changes in yourself? Have you had extra time to do projects you've procrastinated doing? Have you pursued any creative endeavors? Did you read? Did you exercise or go outdoors more often? Were you able to convince your roommates or family to abstain from television with you? Did you miss watching television? Did you notice any difference in your emotional state? Were you more aware of the media's tactics in advertising in magazines, newspapers and radio? Will you return to your regular television viewing or abstain from television for longer? Why or why not? Will you turn it on for shorter periods of time or eliminate certain types of programs? What void does television fill for you? What specific benefits would you receive by keeping it off?

Television is a great tool for living in a fog. Many people watch television out of boredom. People can live vicariously through make-believe characters, while forgetting their real-life struggles. Horrible situations that they don't want to face can be forgotten in this pretend world. But they also avoid finding their own real-life happiness. It can become an addiction for many people, just like alcohol or drugs. And the beauty of this addiction is that they have a never ending supply of their drug. One show plays after the next. Enticing previews of the lineup for the evening or the upcoming week are replayed often so that they are well-informed of their viewing options.

Many talented artists do not watch or own a television. Release your Complacent Scoundrel by limiting or eliminating your exposure to television.

Exercise

To release the Complacent Scoundrel, set your body in motion. Go for a walk or a run. Go for a bike ride. Join an aerobics or martial arts class. Do yoga. Garden. Swim. Climb the stairs. Clean your home. Play.

Exercise reduces stress. It decreases our negative perception of things. It releases endorphins and physically helps us to feel better. A good sweat will release toxins from our bodies. Our metabolism will rise. Our internal organs will be stimulated. Psychologically, it helps us feel a sense of accomplishment that we have done something positive for ourselves. It also gives us a break in the day.

For Complacent Scoundrels who have been sedentary for years, the idea of exercise may not seem like fun. You may have a preconceived notion or recent memory of exercise being painful and leaving you miserable for days. But recall the exhilarating moments of physical activity in your childhood, perhaps remembering that feeling you had when you first learned how to ride a bike. Or remember a time when you held a bat or a racket and made contact with a ball in tennis, baseball, softball, racquetball or golf. Remember when you scored for your team. Remember the feeling of running in a tall field or wading in a stream. Remember when you did something amazing by moving your body.

Change your perception from the mentality that exercise is agonizing to the reality that exercise can be fun and rewarding. Embrace the belief that exercise can give you a great deal of enjoyment. Two important keys to making exercise fun are beginning a program gently and discovering what activities you like.

Most sedentary adults who begin an exercise program lack true desire. They believe that they *should* exercise. Many have a weight loss goal in mind as they torture themselves by doing too much, too soon. Many carry shame about being overweight and sedentary and don't ask other people for help. When they don't see the immediate results they had hoped for after a week or two of intense diet and exercise, they become defeated and quit.

The first problem with this scenario is that they are hurting themselves by shocking their physical, mental and emotional bodies with intense exercise and extreme dieting. The second problem is that they want immediate gratification. It is unlikely that the ten or twenty pounds they want to shed will disappear in the first two weeks. The third problem is that they have no desire to exercise – it is merely a thought that they *should*. They may think they *should* exercise because it is supposed to be good for them. Or because their doctors suggested it. Or because friends or family members are concerned about their health. Or because it would make them more mobile in their daily lives. True desire is a key to incorporating a new habit. Without this desire, their internal motivation is low and it places an even greater emphasis on the numbers on the scale. True desire plus unyielding belief gives you the power to climb mountains!

The fourth problem is not seeking a support system. They opt to do it alone. When the going gets tough, the program ends because no one else is there to keep them accountable and motivated. The fifth problem is mind-set. They go into a new program thinking it will be hard, perhaps remembering past attempts at starting new exercise programs. They make few, if any, changes from past failed attempts to adhere to a program. The only thing that might be different than the past, however, is beginning even more intensely, shocking the body even more and increasing the risk of injury and burnout.

Here are some ideal ways to begin and continue an exercise program:

- **Begin with five to thirty minutes of exercise four to five times each week.** If you typically don't exercise, aim for five to ten minutes. Walking around the neighborhood is usually the easiest choice for a beginner exerciser. The goal here is to make exercise a habit in your daily life. Don't focus on weight loss at this point. If you feel nervous about your neighbors seeing you out walking, go at a time when few people will be outside, like early in the morning or late in the evening.

- **Exercise at a pace that equals a brisk walk.** Aim for an intensity level that feels like you are at fifty to seventy percent intensity rather than ninety or one hundred percent.

- **Exercise in the morning.** You will typically have more energy and fewer excuses in the morning than later in the day. By completing your workout in the morning, you will feel successful the rest of the day. If you do not look forward to exercise and you wait until evening, you carry a sense of dread with you all day long.

- **Get a buddy.** A friend, family member, significant other, neighbor, personal trainer or group exercise class can all be great sources of support. Have several of these support systems in place when you begin. The larger your support network, the larger your support. As your program gets tougher, you will have people to continue motivating you as well as keeping you accountable to your program.

- **Don't complicate things.** If you are beginning an exercise program, exercise. If you are beginning a diet program, eat healthier. Don't begin both at the same time. It is overwhelming and more likely that you will fail at both. Beginning an intense exercise program and drastically reducing your calories is comparable to adopting triplets and four puppies. Both scenarios result in a difficult, unnecessary adjustment period.

- **Eat more vegetables.** You don't need to change anything in your diet initially, but if you want to improve it in one simple way – eat more vegetables and your stomach will have less room for junk.

- **Think positively.** Your mind is more powerful than your body. Getting your mind in shape will make it easier for your body to get in shape.

Change this thought:	To this thought:
"Diets don't work for me."	*"This plan is working for me."*
"I hate exercise."	*"Exercise is enjoyable."*
"My metabolism is slow."	*"My metabolism is getting faster."*
"This is hard."	*"This is getting easier." "This is easy."*
"I hate to sweat."	*"Sweating is good. It releases toxins."*
"I'm not flexible."	*"I am getting more flexible every day."*
"I'm tired."	*"I have energy to do all that I need to do."*
"I can't do this."	*"I can accomplish anything."*
"I can't do this for the rest of my life."	*"I can do this today."*
"I'm not as young as I used to be."	*"I am capable in this moment, at this age."*
"This isn't worth it."	*"Every healthy step I take reaps benefits."*
"I can't lose weight."	*"I am my ideal weight." (visualize it)*

- **Get rid of options.** It is not an option to drive a car and never fill it with gas or get it serviced and maintained. Treat your body like the most precious machine on earth. Just because cheesy, salty snacks exist does not mean you need to put them in your body. Just because no one makes you sleep eight hours or drink water does not mean you don't need adequate amounts of both. Just because no one makes you exercise does not mean it is optional. It's not. Your goal is to move thirty minutes a day, five to six days of the week.

- **Get rid of excuses.** If you want something in your life and it's for your highest good, make it a priority to go after it. Going out to dinner, to a movie, to a bar or watching television are not good reasons for not exercising. Neither is being tired. Formulate and commit to your exercise plans. Eliminate excuses.

- **Setbacks are a key to change.** When one happens, get back on track without burdening yourself with shame, guilt or judgment. Also, do not shame yourself when you are unmotivated to exercise. Let the past stay in the past and move on to the present. Every week, it is okay to take a day or two off or allow for a shorter or less intense workout. But make a pledge to yourself that the next day you will work out. Have a plan that you will execute the following day and exercise in the morning to make *certain* it happens. Be consistent with your workouts. Stay with the present moment and the healthiest option for you right NOW.

It is much easier to adhere to an exercise program when you find something you enjoy. This may take a while, even up to a year or more, so in the beginning, choose activities that are at least tolerable to you. Remember to get rid of excuses and options.

Joining a class or a group that meets on a regular basis is a great way to stay accountable during the early stages of an exercise program. A class can help to distract you from being bored and can help to motivate you when you know other people in the class. It is also much harder to quit during a session when you are in a group setting.

If nothing physically active sounds like fun and you feel intimidated about being in a group setting, choose a simple activity like walking or biking. If you haven't exercised for years, start with a five minute walk once a day. Every day, no matter how much you don't want to go for that walk, find it within yourself to *begin* that walk. If there happens to be a day where you could not find it within yourself to go on a five minute walk, accept that you had a setback. Forgive yourself. Be certain to go for a walk the next morning.

After two weeks of consistent five minute walks, try ten minutes. Increase your time and your intensity when you feel you are ready. Don't go too fast or too hard, but don't stay with a slow, easy five or ten minute walk forever, either. Find a nice balance that gets your heart beating faster and puts a smile on your face.

You can also add in a component of joy to exercise:

- Visualize yourself doing the activity with joy. Stay positive in your thinking and see yourself enjoying the activity.

- Add in a joyful component to the activity. Use the time spent exercising to listen to music, walk a dog or spend time with a child. Take advantage of the quiet time to meditate or solve a problem.

- Make a conscious choice to be happy and enjoy the activity. Let your mind dictate your mood.

- Reward yourself with something that makes you joyful. Enjoy your reward after you've exercised for the day or the week. This should be non-food related, like reading a book, watching a movie, taking a bubble bath or getting a massage. Extrinsic motivators can be as helpful as seeing and feeling the internal health benefits.

The first program with which I stayed consistent was running, despite many grueling months in the beginning. In fact, I struggled most of the first year. But at some point, I found the runners' high. I realized that running is not merely physical; it is an activity that positively shifts the mind, body and spirit by connecting to the Universe.

Although the beautiful, enjoyable feelings that running brought me did not occur in those first few months, something in me trusted that the difficult stage would pass and great rewards awaited me on the other side. So I kept running.

There were many days in the early years that I did not want to exercise and I honored that for a day or two, but I refused to give myself an option or an excuse beyond that. My health and the joy of moving my body gracefully became too important to dismiss.

While exercising, believe that exhilarating moments await you. We are physical beings. Our bodies are temples. We must treat them as such. Find whatever physical activity is the most tolerable – or even enjoyable – for you and go do it!

Recognize and credit yourself when you seize the motivation and reap the benefits of moving your body divinely.

Nutrition

Processed, high calorie foods are more visible to us than in the past. There are numerous coffee shops and convenience stores lining the streets, more vending machines in buildings and more food options at businesses that have no focus on food, such as gas stations and pharmacies. Healthy convenient foods, such as apples, oranges, bananas and carrots are not items placed at eye level in checkout lanes. Rather, candy bars and bags of chips are stocked near cashiers, ready to be impulsively purchased.

So, is this the reason why people have become collectively obese?

Certainly that is not the only reason. Along with a greater visibility of high calorie foods, there has been an enormous increase in the quantity of food served, an increase in consumption of sodas, juices, caffeinated and flavored drinks and a general exodus from natural foods to processed ones.

Less exercise, especially in jobs which require minimal physical labor, combined with quantities of high calorie foods, contributes to obesity. There is no riddle to be solved here. No more studies need to be done. It does not really matter how or why humans have become so grossly overweight.

The questions that do need to be answered now are: How do we, as individuals, move into patterns of eating healthier? How do we get back to the basics? How do we release our Complacent Scoundrels that are okay with eating whatever is easiest, most convenient and tastes the best, to eating the very best for our bodies' needs?

As people begin to value themselves more and find fulfillment within themselves rather than in food, they move away from eating "junk." Once this mind-set has changed, it typically is solidified for life. Stress is one of the few things that can upset a balanced, mindful diet. When we fall out of harmony within ourselves, we again look to external fixes to regain internal balance. This never works. A piece of chocolate cake will not resolve a bad day. Exercise, conscious breathing, meditation, spending time with the elements, journaling and direct communication with other people are far better options to dealing with stress. We want to avoid having an unhealthy, adverse relationship to food where we abuse our bodies to deal with emotional distress.

Get rid of the idea of "dieting." Make healthy changes that can be supported for life. Avoid the "should" mentality. Avoid the scale (unless you use it as a biofeedback tool and not as a way to linger in self-disapproval). Two individuals with completely different body types can step on the scale and weigh the same. This is because lean body mass versus fat mass is not considered on most scales and the ones that have a fat reading are often inaccurate. Instead of hopping on the scale, look for cues that say, *I'm fit. I'm healthy. I'm strong.*

We need to ask our bodies what they want. We can no longer eat with our minds, our memories, our taste buds or our emotions. We need to make plans and prepare food in advance, so that we have healthy snacks and meals available. We need to eat in the present moment, slowly and consciously. We need to savor the foods we love with joy rather than guilt and shame. We need to eat on a regular basis, so we are not starving ourselves at any point in the day, putting us at the whim of eating convenient, processed food or binging to counter our hunger pains.

There is no single diet that will work well for every living human. We have specific needs dependent on our body types. The best solution is to listen to your body. Choose organic fruits, vegetables, legumes and whole grains. If you're not sure if a food is right for your body, hold the food in your hand or hold your hand over the food. As you hold the food, does your body feel weaker? Do you feel heavy or tired? Does your pulse rate begin to increase? If there is any adverse physical reaction to the food, choose something else to eat. Release past experiences with certain foods and past knowledge. Don't feel that any particular food must be good for you because it is a healthy food or you've been taught that it is necessary for you. Let your body, not your mind, decide.

Food addictions and emotional eating can be two of the greatest challenges in a lifetime. Because food is involved in nearly every social event and is considered by most to be a pleasurable part of life, it is something we need to be conscious of several times each day. The following section, Get Conscious at the Dinner Table, will further help Complacent Scoundrels with this issue.

Get Conscious at the Dinner Table

Imagine coming home after a long day of work. Low on energy and feeling stressed, you proceed directly to the kitchen for a quick boost. You open a bag of tortilla chips and a jar of salsa, grab a couple handful of nuts and drink half a can of soda before you're ready to start contemplating dinner.

Sound familiar? Many of us come home famished and nibble at a few things before we've even thought about what we're doing and what our bodies really want to eat. It's a way to unwind after a stressful day. In the above example, this habit added six hundred and ten calories to your daily caloric intake (one hundred and thirty = one serving of chips, forty-five calories = six tablespoons of salsa, about three hundred and sixty calories = two ounces of fancy mixed nuts, seventy-five calories = a half can of soda). Those six hundred and ten calories can make a big difference in the big picture of your life.

Looking at this scenario, we see that it may not be the healthiest way for us to relax. Clearly it is time to integrate a better solution into our lives.

Step One: Transition

Before entering your home, sit for a few moments in your car, on your lawn or on your front steps. Take a few deep breaths. Allow your body to relax. As little as ten breaths will bring a closure to your work day and prepare you for entering your home with more peaceful energy. Breathe for five minutes or more to gain more clarity in the present moment. You will open your front door with a different perspective than you would have had without the transition.

Step Two: Check in with your Mood

How has your day been going? Are you happy? Tired? Stressed? Anxious? Excited? Irritated? Are you content with your work day? With your co-workers? Did you have fun? Are you dreading going back to work? Was there any situation you wish you could have handled differently? Was there anything you wished you had said but didn't? Are there any problems you need to resolve in the next twelve hours?

If there is something weighing on you, take a moment now to recognize the issue. Take one mental step toward resolving it. For example, you may have a presentation to give next week and you're already nervous about it. Recognize your anxiety. Understand that it is warranted and valuable. Commit to taking twenty minutes after dinner to work on your presentation. Maybe you can brainstorm ideas while going for a walk or taking a soothing bath. Even though you may not be able to solve the issue now, dedicate a moment to it and take one step toward its resolution, to avoid spending the next four hours in a beaten down, frustrated mood.

Step Three: Check in with your Body

What is your body, *not your mind,* craving? Ask it. What do you need right now and how much of it do you need? Have you been craving carrots all day because your eyes have been feeling strained? Have you felt congested and your body is screaming for a good, spicy curry? Take a moment and let your body decide what dinner is going to be. Don't let your mind override this decision.

Step Four: Sit

Remember the six hundred and ten calories of chips, salsa, nuts and soda consumed to help wind down the day? Those were all eaten while standing. The body barely registered that it was ingesting food even though a large amount of calories were eaten.

If you are ravenous when you come home and must eat something before you cook dinner, take a few moments of conscious contemplation before grabbing the first thing you see. Plain fruits and vegetables may not be the best answer for you right now if your body needs some fat at this point in the day. Carrots and two tablespoons of a high calorie, high fat dip, such as hummus or ranch dressing might be a perfect solution. Fix yourself a plate of carrots and dip and sit at the table.

Sitting and eating allows your body to rest and focus on your food. If you are going to eat something, even a snack, take your exact portion – NOT THE ENTIRE BAG OR CONTAINER – to the dining room table.

Or better yet, head out to a comfortable chair on the porch or to a nice, shady spot outside. The further away you are from the next serving, the less likely you will be to have another serving. Since it takes approximately twenty minutes for your body to register that it is full, you'll often find the first serving was plenty.

Step Five: Pause and Get Conscious

Mealtime is not a time to pay bills, do homework, read, check the Internet, watch television or do anything that distracts you from eating. Meals can be spent talking with your family or friends, allowing the conversation and the company to add to the pleasure of your meal. Keep the conversation positive.

Do you like to eat good food? Then sit and eat it. Do nothing else. Just eat. Don't distract yourself from enjoying this pleasure. You deserve a delicious meal. Don't think about the work you need to do. Don't think about your stressful day. Focus on the meal sitting before you. Enjoy the colors, aromas, textures, temperatures and tastes. Think happy, loving thoughts and let your food nourish you. Eat slowly and chew your food. Set down your fork or spoon between bites. Make every meal a special time for you. Be grateful for your meal.

As you are getting conscious with your food, ask yourself a few questions about your meal. Was it made with love? Did you make healthy choices? Are you listening to your body and giving it what it needs? Is it a balanced meal? Does it include vegetables? Is it organic?

If you answered no to two or more of the above questions, ask yourself why. Uncover the reason why you are not treating your body like a temple. If you were hosting a dinner party tonight, would you be serving your guests the same dinner you are eating, or would you make them something better? If you wouldn't serve your guests the same dinner, then why are you eating it? Is it because of convenience? That's not a good enough answer. Uncover the reason why you are not feeding yourself as though you are a king or queen worthy of the finest foods. Treat yourself as the person you most admire and most love not only by what you feed yourself, but in everything you do.

2
Delayed Gratification Scoundrel

Many mature Westerners harbor a Delayed Gratification Scoundrel inside of them. Rather than choosing to be happy now, they choose to look forward to happiness at some later date or time. This future time might be when it's five o'clock, the weekend, summer vacation, a winter holiday, when they are a certain age, when they are married, when they own a house, when they have children, when they pay off their mortgage, when their children are grown or when they retire.

Many Delayed Gratification Scoundrels are locked into the mindset of retirement and enjoying that new phase of their lives. Unfortunately, many Delayed Gratification Scoundrels either do not live long enough to experience much, if any, of their retirement or they have health issues that preclude them from fulfilling the dreams and plans they had in their younger years.

Given the choice of getting a single scoop of ice cream today or a double decker tomorrow, Delayed Gratification Scoundrels would wait until tomorrow. But tomorrow might not find them with the same craving for ice cream. More likely than not, the ice cream gets forgotten altogether.

This may not be a bad thing. Our inner child demands instant gratification. Obviously if we always give in to the whims of our inner child, we may lack self-discipline. Without discipline, we may not get very far on our life paths. We may find ourselves without purpose, satisfying one craving after another with no end in sight. But

51

with that self-discipline, must come content. Being well-disciplined and unhappy, does not make an enjoyable life journey.

There are various times in life when planning for tomorrow, such as investing time or money in business, real estate, education and other long-term plans, can be a positive thing. It is a wonderful mentality for good parenting, keeping children focused on one task and then on a reward: "Clean your room and then you can play." It also works well for adults when there is a task we don't want to complete – treat yourself to a movie after finishing your taxes.

Delaying your gratification becomes a problem when you never choose what will make you happy now or when you sacrifice present happiness for what may never come to fruition.

Happiness for Delayed Gratification Scoundrels remains in the future. Because they continually delay their happiness, they aren't able to experience those moments of happiness when they arrive because they are already looking forward to the next "happiness milestone." (This aspect of the Delayed Gratification Scoundrel can also be categorized as the Forward-Thinking Scoundrel.) Chances are, if they aren't happy now, they won't be happy later, either. Unable to experience contentment in the present, they remain unhappy.

Instead of waiting until tomorrow to go swimming, go swimming today. That is what your heart yearns to do. It could be raining tomorrow. However, if going swimming today means you'll have to stay up half the night finishing a present you are making for a friend's birthday tomorrow, then obviously it would be better to go swimming tomorrow and get a good night's sleep.

You could also go for a quick, five-minute swim today and go for a longer swim tomorrow. You could ask another friend to help you finish making the birthday present and you both could go swimming today. You could swim today and wake up early to finish the present. When you are weighing your options, make sure you know what *all* your options are.

In order to create joy in our lives, we must make peace with our inner child and our mature adult. We need to find balance within the present moment and tomorrow. Much of this balance can occur by equally listening to our heads and our hearts. Our inner child reigns in our heart; our mature adult reigns in our mind. Allow both to have their say. Weigh all your options and make the most balanced choice between your head and your heart.

More than anything, for all of our scoundrels to be released, we must *strive for contentment within the moment*. What is the point of delaying your happiness? You will not earn a medal for it. We are meant to be living in *joy*. There is no need to plan ahead to experience that joy. Experience it now. In the moment. That means, regardless of any decision that gets made, we are happy *right now*. If we go swimming now, we are happy now. If we go swimming tomorrow, we are happy now and we will be equally happy tomorrow. If we finish making a birthday present, we are happy now and happy when we offer the gift. If we go to sleep early, we are happy. If we go to sleep two hours later than usual, we are happy.

Following the heart from a place of sincerity, purity and joy is almost always the best decision for Delayed Gratification Scoundrels. You do not need to wait a single second for happiness to arrive. Find it within yourself. Within this moment.

Comments you might hear from Delayed Gratification Scoundrels:

> *"Only four more days 'till Friday!"*
> *"Only thirteen years 'till retirement."*
> *"I'll wait to open that package until I've sorted through all the bills."*
> *"No dessert unless you eat your vegetables."*
> *"I'll wait to see if that goes on sale."*

If you OBSERVE and VERIFY the Delayed Gratification Scoundrel in your life, EXAMINE the following:

1. How has the Delayed Gratification Scoundrel helped you?
2. How has it negatively affected you?
3. To the best of your recollection, when were you first introduced to the Delayed Gratification Scoundrel? Is this a family, cultural or societal scoundrel you consciously or unconsciously

accepted as your own?

4. What are some examples of how you've been a Delayed Gratification Scoundrel in the past week?

5. Ask yourself at different times during the week, during different tasks, if there is anything you would rather be doing. If there is, can you do that instead of what you are doing? Keep questioning yourself for months or even years. The goal with this line of questioning is to get to a place where you never want to be doing anything else than what you are currently doing. This is a great way to realize when the Delayed Gratification Scoundrel is gone.

6. On a scale of one to ten, ten being the best, how would you rate your overall level of satisfaction and happiness in life?

7. Write a list of ways you have delayed your happiness in the past. Now write a list of ways that you can attain instant gratification. In the next several months, find the balance between instant and delayed gratification. Compromise between the two.

8. What is one thing you can do TODAY to have gratification and happiness in your life TODAY?

RELEASE Delayed Gratification Scoundrel Mentality with the following Affirmations:

- ॐ *I deserve all that I desire.*
- ॐ *I desire all that I deserve.*
- ॐ *I deserve to live the life I choose to lead.*
- ॐ *I choose to be happy now.*
- ॐ *I live in a limitless reality.*
- ॐ *I accept the abundance of the Universe now.*
- ॐ *My happiness is important to me today.*
- ॐ *I listen to my heart.*
- ॐ *I am in awe of my life as it stands right now.*
- ॐ *I am balanced between work and play.*
- ॐ *I revel in the ebb and flow of life.*

Play

Playing is a key principle to joy, especially for Delayed Gratification Scoundrels who allow their mature adult to be their boss.

Think about how you played as a child. Growing up, you may have loved stickers and markers. Maybe you played baseball, created stories and designed crafts. Perhaps you still do these things today, but to a much lesser extent.

Maybe you enjoy painting, carpentry, restoring antiques or cooking. Maybe one of your favorite hobbies is building doll houses or even playing in them.

What elements from childhood can you bring back into your adult life? What elements have never gone away, but haven't been indulged in lately?

Take time out of your day to play. Do things that you enjoy, that entertain and excite you. Give yourself permission to act silly and laugh. If you need an excuse to be silly, playing with children or pets is a great way to act goofy. It gives you an opportunity to use a silly voice, make silly faces and play with toys you normally wouldn't touch.

It is important to play and laugh. Laughing and being silly with friends are fundamental to playtime. Skipping, doing cartwheels, sprinting up a set of stairs at the park, playing a harmless practical joke, flirting, coloring with crayons, finger painting and dressing up for a costume party are all great ways to play. Climb a tree. Hoola hoop. Somersault. Swim. Spend the day in your underwear and watch cartoons. Enjoy a beautiful sunset — not from behind the window of a house or car, but sitting or standing in nature. Bask in the sun. Play darts or any other game and don't keep score. Wear ribbons in your hair or crazy neckties. Wear orange and purple together with polka dots. Get out of your own way and leave your serious mind-set behind you.

Just remember to play.

Because the more serious our lives become, the more necessary it is to play.

"Edith's" motto was, "Do your worst first." She always believed in getting the bad out of the way so that you could then enjoy the good. The problem with this motto was that at eighty years old, she had failed to do much beyond "the worst." Dealing with cancer, her children encouraged her to "Do your best first." They laid out her paint supplies and crafts on the dining room table so that she could spend every morning doing what she truly loved. With this new motto and new action, her health improved greatly.

Somewhere along the way, we have become mature adults and responsible citizens. We have let Delayed Gratification Scoundrels take over our happiness and we've decided we'll wait until some magical day like retirement to take it back. What is the point of "growing up" if it means you can't have toys and playtime? What is the point of becoming responsible and earning a decent salary if it enslaves you to a boring life? Why would anyone want to leave behind roller coasters, cotton candy and cartoons because we feel we've become too mature?

Even the most evolved spiritual masters in India play games and jokes and love to laugh. In Sanskrit, the word for play is *"leela."* Every day we can engage in our own *leela* and have fun doing it.

It is easy to get angry when "bad" things happen to us. Life is enjoyable when we can enjoy the humor in things. We can learn the lessons in things, but we can also have a great big belly laugh about them, too.

One of my best friends and I were having a difficult morning on vacation in India. This was the first time either of us had been at an ashram, a religious hermitage, and we were stretched in many ways, as was our friendship. Sitting in the beautiful garden before dawn, stars twinkled above us and the Ganges River hummed below us. The slight breeze felt refreshing, yet the air between me and my friend felt suffocating. My friend angrily stomped away – only to end up walking in a perfect circle right back to where she had been sitting.

We burst into laughter. The humor of the moment was absolutely divine. We breathed more easily and became calmer and more rational. We enjoyed the *leela* that was playing before us.

Experience *leela* in your life. Add more joy in your life through playing. Nurture your inner child.

Do your best first.

Dance

Another simple task, or is it? If it's so terribly simple, why do many people do their best to avoid it? Or why do they only do it after they've had a drink or two? Millions of people across the globe dance with a meaningful purpose. People dance in celebration, dance as an art form, dance to attract a mate, dance in competition, and dance for ceremonial purposes.

Children dance freely all the time. They are very willing to dance in front of others. Their inhibition is low and their appreciation for attention and desire to entertain is high. If you are a Delayed Gratification Scoundrel attempting to regain your inner child, dancing is one of best things you can do.

Find your own meaningful purpose to dance. Dance because you are in a beautiful human body. Dance because you can. Crank up your favorite tunes. Put on rock music, heavy metal, classical, reggae, Latin music or whatever suits your mood.

Close the door to your bedroom. Close the drapes in your living room. Give yourself whatever privacy you need. Allow your body to express itself in whatever way feels natural and fun. Don't criticize yourself; don't allow others to criticize you – just dance. Dance in front of a mirror or close your eyes and feel the rhythm of the music. Be confident in your moves.

Celebrate yourself. Raise your arms and get your heart pumping. Smile. Glisten inside and out with the divinity that is your true nature. Let your happiness soar with your movements. Dance. Dance. Dance!

Live in Awe

I took my nephew to the zoo when he was two years old. We stood behind the wire-linked fence watching the buffalo on the other side. At least I thought we were both watching the buffalo. When he started giggling and pointing right in front of him, I turned to see what had captured his attention. In the midst of a fifteen hundred pound buffalo, he was entranced by a leaf fluttering on a branch in front of him.

I crinkled up my forehead with curiosity. Why wasn't he looking at the magnificent creature before us? How could a leaf win over a buffalo?

And then I stooped down to his eye level and took a second look at the leaf. It twisted and twirled around with a flair that made me question how much longer it would remain attached on its branch. It certainly seemed inconsequential and commonplace next to a buffalo, but it was putting on its own show.

Sometimes it takes the eyes of a two-year-old to remind us of the magic that all things possess. Remember when you were a child. Go back to the age of three or four, or the earliest age you can recall. Did you ever lie in bed for twenty minutes dreading to get up and face the day? Most likely not. You had fun things to do, like playing outside, watching cartoons, drawing pictures, inventing friends and stories and games and toys. Life was fun and exciting and you were the creator of it all.

Life is a far cry from that now, isn't it? Even if you have a free day, you usually spend it doing chores you put off during the week. You are a grown up now. You have responsibilities. And there's nothing much fun about that, is there?

Yes, there is.

Without quitting your job or rearranging your lifestyle, you can start to bring back that sense of awe you had as a child.

Begin to pay attention to the beautiful details in life, not only the big picture, as adults tend to do. Notice the delicate dancing leaves, the rays of sunlight poking through the clouds, the ants building their hills and the chirping of crickets. Stop moving full speed ahead through your life. Pause to bathe your senses in the little things that you once found marvelous.

Years ago, I lived in California, near the Mojave Desert. When I first arrived there, I thought I had moved to a desert wasteland where everything looked brown and dead. I appreciated the warm climate, but little else. Tumbleweed drifted across the roads. The smell of dust permeated the air and quickly covered everything in my apartment.

While living there, I had many opportunities to travel. Each time I returned, I saw something I hadn't noticed in the past. Something I began to appreciate for the first time. Something that said home. I grew to adore the hardiness of the Joshua tree, got excited about the jack rabbits and coyotes that darted about the desert, and discovered the subtle differences in the hues of browns and greens that colored the landscape. I grew in awe of what I had formerly thought ugly.

The desert didn't change. My recognition and awe of the details did.

As you begin to appreciate the little things in your environment, recognize the little things in yourself, like how good your posture is, how quickly you can type, how your sense of humor makes people laugh. Enjoy each thing inside and outside of yourself. Recognize the interconnectedness between the internal and external. Begin to understand the relationships between things. Allow yourself to move into this awareness.

And allow yourself to be in awe of life.

Discover a Neutral Balance

To live in ultimate joy, we must live in a neutral balance. This idea of being neutral can be applied in dozens of different ways, such as:

- in relationships
- in sex
- in jobs
- with projects
- in our living situation
- with our mode (vehicle) of transportation
- in music
- in money
- in food
- in the time of the day
- in the day of the week
- in the month of the year
- in the season
- in the temperature
- in our age
- in our race
- in our looks
- in our status
- in our fitness level
- in our family
- in our friends
- in animals
- in our attachment to anything

In any situation, we can be pulled in two opposite directions. But instead of moving to an extreme, be creative. Choose any of the myriad of options that lie in the middle ground. This is one of the biggest lessons for Delayed Gratification Scoundrels to learn: you have many options and they can all be wonderful. For example, many people tend to dislike Mondays and love Saturdays, while feeling indifferent toward Wednesdays. But in order to live in constant contentment, we need to be in the neutral zone, where every day offers as much opportunity and joy as another. We do not need to categorize one day as good or another day as bad, we can simply have them all be lovely days.

From the neutral zone, we don't have to categorize anything as good or bad, positive or negative, black or white, hard or easy, happy or sad. We can rid ourselves of dualistic thinking. Every season, temperature, age, food, animal and relationship can be viewed without bias. So often, a story is told and a response is made, such as, "That's too bad" or "That will be a hard thing to do." Unless we are omniscient regarding past, present and future, there is no way to have a valid assessment on anything that occurs. We don't know at present if something is "bad" or "hard." Allow it to be its own experience without the need to categorize it. Experiencing people, things and situations as they are – in an authentic, non-judgmental way – allows us the best opportunity to live in the neutral zone.

"Jonathan" learned this lesson of neutrality quickly while working at a retreat center in exchange for his room and board. One of his jobs was to shovel horse manure. Another of his duties was to tend the magnificent flower garden at the center. He found he had no preference for either job; he was perfectly content with both. This is the aim for which we strive – being content, but not complacent with whatever comes our way.

The following internal struggle details the process of finding neutrality. "Carl," a vegetarian, finds himself dreaming of meat night after night and craving meat during the day. He continually denies this desire because he has been dogmatic in his vegetarian practice for fifteen years. He does not want to contribute to the slaughter of a living creature through his consumption of meat. But Carl lives with a constant pull toward meat. His body and mind are relentless in this desire.

How can he move into a neutral position regarding his own consumption of meat? He formerly avoided it. Now he is contemplating becoming a carnivore again. Depending on the amount of meat Carl may now choose to eat, he could be moving from one extreme to another and miss the neutral zone altogether. To linger in the neutral zone, he could instead choose to eat just one meal of meat or even one *piece* of meat. When he indulges in that meat, he can reflect with gratitude on the animal that was sacrificed. After his meal, he may continue his vegetarian lifestyle for another fifteen years.

Or perhaps he decides to eat meat one time each year or one time per month. Or Carl simply listens to his body and eats meat when his body says it is time. Without judgment, he finds the middle ground. Maybe in a year or two, he returns to being a strict vegetarian. Maybe he doesn't.

Perhaps Carl is not even meant to eat meat, but instead he is simply to explore the action or concept of eating meat or why some humans choose to eat it. Perhaps the craving has merely manifested to remind him not to judge those who eat meat or to remind him not to react when he discovers meat is being served at a dinner party.

Ideally, when we make a choice in the neutral zone, it is a choice made without judgment for ourselves or others. We simply and calmly check in with ourselves and our higher power and make the best decision. We can allow that decision to change when it needs to. We are continually learning and growing. What is right for us one moment may be inappropriate for us at a different moment and vice versa.

Sitting in a neutral zone also means sitting in a zone void of reaction or emotion. We merely take in the information through observation, as if this situation has occurred to *any* human being, rather than having happened to us. All sides of the situation are seen from everyone's viewpoint without any judgment or bias. It is processed in its own way and time. We either take necessary, rational action or we file the information for later. Releasing the fact that we were hurt in a situation, releases the ego from barging into the situation and taking control like an angry child. The benefit of this is that we become rational, mature adults that operate from a place of objectivity and compassion and offer fair solutions that make sense for everyone involved.

For example, "Tina" discovers her friend, "Alyssa" has been gossiping about her. If Tina is acting outside of the neutral zone, she may react to this discovery by immediately calling Alyssa and heatedly demanding an explanation. Alyssa may tell her she did not gossip and offer a weak explanation for what she had said, leaving Tina in a greater outrage, even angrier than when she initially heard about the gossip. She may fire back angry words before ending the phone call.

If Tina approaches this situation from a neutral zone, she would take whatever appropriate amount of time she needed in order to be able to have a rational conversation. She then calmly asks her friend for an explanation. Alyssa may still tell her she did not gossip and offer her weak explanation, but in this scenario Tina listens without reacting. She has already removed her emotions from the situation. Tina tells Alyssa why what she is saying is inaccurate and ends the phone call.

In both situations, the outcome remains roughly the same. One friend feels the other friend gossiped. The friend who has gossiped does not confess. It doesn't matter if Tina operates in the neutral zone or not, the situation and the apparent outcome up to this point does not change. So, what is the benefit of operating from the neutral zone? When Tina is in the neutral zone, she can function from an unattached, unemotional place. She is not ruffled by Alyssa's weak explanations. She remains in a place of contentment despite whatever her friend or anyone else may do.

Being in the neutral zone also means being in a space of nonattachment. It means being unattached to the outcomes of situations, things and people. It is much easier to be living in contentment and joy when things can roll off our shoulders. We can find ourselves in a neutral position as new people, things or opportunities enter our lives or old ones exit. In order to do this, we must not heap an abundance of love or attention on any one person or thing. We instead can appreciate everyone and everything in our lives. We can meet them and add to their lives and they can add to ours; things can remain indifferent, we can learn from them or they can learn from us. Gratitude and nonattachment, combined with trust in the Universe that we are always safe and protected, help us not to react to the little things in life that may otherwise pull us away from contentment.

This does not mean suppressing your emotions. If you experience sadness or romantic love, honor it. Express it. Move forward.

By releasing attachment to everyone and everything, little by little, the emotional roller coasters in life become smooth. Non-attachment allows for synchronization in our lives. One moment flows into the next. One day flows into another. The need for drama is released from our lives and replaced with harmony and the continual craving for balance. We move closer to living in the blissful reality in which we were meant to be living. We embrace our natural divinity and our true power.

Being in neutral also means operating with patience. It means we are not imposing our will over the divine plan of the Universe. It means stating our desires and releasing them, along with our attachment to their outcomes. It allows the Universe to prepare things for us and to operate in its divine timeline. In letting go, we open ourselves to receive.

This neutral zone exists between patience and aggression. It is important that we don't wait for things that we feel led to act upon. It is equally important that we aren't overly aggressive and impose our will on situations. How do we find that neutral zone?

If we find ourselves presented with opportunities that we know would be in everyone's best interest to accept, but instead we wait, as Delayed Gratification Scoundrels are prone to do, we are being inactive to the detriment of everybody involved. We are hiding behind our fear and calling it patience. This inactivity is a waste of time for us and for others. Be prepared to act upon what needs to be done and is in your capacity to do.

The other side of this situation is continually pushing and struggling when we know there is an easier and simpler way to accomplish something. Look to find the result of what it is you are seeking to accomplish. Who benefits? If it is you alone or mostly you, then it may also be a good time to step back and reevaluate your action. When we meet with resistance time and time again, we need to look within ourselves and to our higher power to see if we should proceed or wait. When we know within ourselves that we must take a step back, allow that to happen so that everything has its proper time and space to realign. We must be prepared to wait.

Listen to your intuition. Look for signs and the synchronization of events. Look for simplicity. Ask yourself if you are balanced between patience and action. Readjust your plan as needed — acting upon what can easily be taken care of, waiting for those things outside your control to arrive in their right time.

Being in neutral means living in balance. It means we have balance between work and play. Between being with others and being alone. Between moving and stillness. Between being serious and enjoying humor. And in attaining this balance, we find continuity among all things because we operate from a place of contentment. From here, all paths of energy will be flowing smoothly and serenely. And when we step into the world, our internal harmony will remain unshakable.

Detach

There may be times in our lives when we find ourselves attached to people, situations, outcomes, animals and things. Despair is certain to find you once these things are removed, even for a short time, or never given to you in the first place. It is a wonderful thing to be pleasantly surprised by the great acting, the unique plotline or the fabulous special effects of a movie you know nothing about rather than have great expectations for a disappointing movie.

Keeping yourself detached from things is a beautiful way to remain content. It is when we become attached that we are content based on the world around us rather than remaining grounded and maintaining a constant level of contentment. When we attach to outcomes, to people, to situations and to material objects, we allow our emotional state to waiver. We become people who react rather than people who act and choose. We become victims rather than leaders of our own destinies.

Let's say you've been dreaming of owning a new couch. You save your money for months and have picked the perfect couch. You buy the couch and position it beautifully in your home with all the right decorating touches surrounding the couch. It becomes your most prized possession and your favorite place in the world. You love to sip your morning tea on the couch, and read and relax on the couch with your cat. Sometimes you sleep on the couch. There is no other couch like it in the world. You are grateful that you own it.

Now imagine that you've gone away for the weekend and return to find your cat threw up a hairball on your couch. You are unable to get the spot out of the couch, but you can flip over the cushion, so it's completely unnoticeable. And then the next day, your cat coughs up a hairball on the other side of the same cushion.

You try every cleaning remedy possible. Despite your best efforts, there is nothing that removes the stains. Your couch is ruined. You are devastated. You no longer enjoy the couch as you once did.

After a few weeks, you stop sighing every time you think about the couch stains. And for the first time in a while you are happy again because you are going to the amusement park with your best friend. You haven't been to this park since you were a teenager, and you have been having a lot of dreams about riding the Ferris wheel. As the day for the park approaches, you get more and more excited. The weather report predicts a pleasant, seventy-six degree day with a low chance of rain.

The morning of your park visit, you wake up happy and eager for your friend to pick you up and whisk you away for a day of much needed fun.

You call your friend to check what time he is picking you up and he tells you he isn't feeling well and he needs to stay home and sleep. Your heart sinks. You are extremely disappointed that you will not spend the day at the park, you will not see your friend, you will not ride the Ferris wheel or do any of the other fun things at the park that you haven't done for years. Your day is ruined. You determine that there is nothing that can happen to change your day and your dashed plans.

In both examples, you allowed external circumstances to affect your mood. You allowed yourself to be attached to the new couch and the trip to the amusement park with your friend. As soon as something unfavorable happened, your happiness was destroyed.

Placing your happiness on external circumstances, people and situations over which you have no control, sets you up for a lifelong series of disappointments. It weakens you. It makes you passive.

The alternative of this is to gain control of your emotions by staying unattached to everything and everyone. This does not mean that you don't care about others. It means that everyone in your world gets treated with the same respect. You give your attention to everyone in the same manner. There are people who may be allowed in your inner circle and there may be others with whom you keep very distinct boundaries, but ultimately, you have the same compassion for everyone.

This also means that you remain unattached to outcomes. You release expectations that certain things will occur and you do not place emotional weight on their occurrence.

Instead you place your faith in the Universe and trust that everything will occur for the highest good. Be conscious and specific in what you want and release your expectation. With the right time and circumstances, your request will manifest in the way that is best for you. Remove your will, your emotions and your attachments. All three of these things will get in your way.

Detachment is one of the most powerful lessons for Delayed Gratification Scoundrels because they place great importance on the outcomes of future events. These scoundrels are devastated when these events fail to occur.

Living with detachment to people and things leaves you with much less pain and suffering. For example, don't assume upon meeting someone that they will become your lifelong friend. Instead, simply enjoy the conversation without expecting a future meeting. Embrace the moment and focus on the present, giving your full attention to the other person. Remain detached from the future — when will you meet this person again, how much longer will you continue talking, etc. It is fine to make future plans, but the focus should be on the present connection, not the possible connection tomorrow.

Aside from being detached to outcomes, we can also be detached from the material world and from the need to be a consumer. Having thirty-three pairs of black heels might be a wonderful luxury to some people, but it becomes a dilemma when deciding which pair best suits an evening dress; having only two pairs makes the decision far easier.

Focused on keeping up with the latest trends, many people often forget about what is going to make their quality of life better and what is not. Moving into a bigger house may seem like a dream come true, but when they discover the extra responsibilities they incur by committing to more space, they realize that maybe life wasn't so bad in their bungalow or one bedroom apartment.

I remember my first backpacking trip. For one month, the only possessions I had access to were the ones in my pack. There were a few things I missed, but for the most part, I was very satisfied and grateful for what I had. Back home, I was able to get rid of a great deal of belongings because I hadn't missed them. Many I had forgotten I even owned and couldn't remember the last time I had used them.

Every long trip I took after that, I was able to detach more and more from my belongings. Soon enough, I was able to reduce possessions to what I truly wanted. And of course, I still had far more than I actually needed, but it was far less than I had before. It helped me to better appreciate the things I kept and later to detach from those things also.

Think about how good you feel when you take a bath or shower after a long day outside. It feels marvelous to rinse that layer of grime and sweat off your body. Imagine that feeling after you've reduced physical excess in your personal space. The new feeling of lightness lifts your spirits in a different way – one that may not be perceptible immediately but will positively affect you forever.

Look at your world and your attachments. Clear the physical attachments first. Have a friend help you if it seems impossible for you. If you're unsure of how much you're ready to release, start with a garbage bag or two for a local charity or a neighborhood garage sale.

Then begin to examine your emotional attachments. Take a moment to think about an outcome to which you've been attached. Release that attachment. Trust that the outcome that is for your highest good will manifest. Notice how different you feel releasing the unnecessary tangible and intangible things you've been holding on to in your life. Trusting in the Universe and recognizing that you have all your needs met in the present moment will make detachment much easier.

Releasing the energy of your attachments will also allow new and better things to come into your life. If we knew a new friendship was waiting for us that exceeded all our desires in a friend, but there was no room for that friendship because we were emotionally unavailable with a demanding and unhealthy friendship that no longer served us, it would be much easier to end the old friendship.

Imagine the goodness awaiting you. Be prepared to receive all that awaits you when you allow space for it to enter.

Add Novelty into Your Life

Part of the reasons why vacations, especially ones far from home, are so nice is because there is so much novelty for us to experience. Our senses get a chance to play. We smell new flowers and spices. We taste new drinks and a variety of different foods. We hear different accents, voices, inflections, words, languages and dialects. We hear new music and sounds in nature. We touch unfamiliar fabrics, objects and plants.

When we're in a new place, *everything* we see is new. Every face is a face we've never seen before. Every road is a road we've never walked down before and may never get the chance to walk down again. Everything becomes candy to our eyes and to our souls.

When we introduce novelty in our lives, life becomes more exciting. This is partly why children are eager to wake up in the morning. There is still so much novelty in their lives at age five. Children continually experience new things. For them, it's hard not to come across things they haven't seen, touched, heard, smelled or done. With millions of stimuli surrounding us daily, there's plenty to experience. Even at age ten, things are still fun and responsibilities are fairly minimal. Little by little, children become aware of what's in their world and new things soon become commonplace. They learn the names of things and their purposes. They come to understand that they will see the same things again and again.

Soon enough, the excitement at seeing a dandelion or hearing a plane overhead becomes less than thrilling. As an adult, they may become annoyed by the presence of either. As we grow, there are less new things to experience in our immediate world. We become attached to our perception of the home we live in and the items inside it. If we were to sleep for two years in a room, we would wake up and not be surprised to see the same items in the space around us. Granted, they might have a good coating of dust on them, but if no one has entered the room in which we were sleeping, little else will have changed.

At thirty or forty, if you live in the same town you grew up in, things become stale and boring. We think the same thoughts every day as we do the same things. Familiar activities activate familiar thoughts and memories. Any wonder why we're using our brains to less than their potential? Every day becomes monotonous and dull when there is no new stimulus. If we aren't bringing novelty into our lives, we grow tired of our existence.

The way many of us have learned to bring novelty back into our lives is through shopping. By continually buying material goods, we can experience the novelty for which we long. One item after another gets brought into our home with practical intention. Years later, many items remain barely used and forgotten.

We start with little things, fun acquisitions that bring us some joy and contentment: nice clothes, jewelry, shoes... We gain a little pleasure from these things and get some positive reinforcement from our peers through their compliments. And thinking we are on the right path to fulfilling our dreams and becoming content, we continue by buying a house, a fancy car, dining in exquisite restaurants, going on cruises and to resorts, buying a boat, a cabin and all the extras needed to make our lives comfortable. We feel the need to acquire bigger, louder stereo systems and wide-screen televisions. We look to find the newest, latest, technologically advanced craze to satisfy us. Thank goodness that we live in a time period of consumerism with amazing technological advancements, so there will always be something newer, better, quicker and flashier.

There are other ways to bring novelty into our lives than by buying new things. Expand your world to shake up what has become ordinary. It need not be anything crazy, just something that you've *never* done before or haven't done for a long while. Take a different route driving home. Listen to different music than you normally do. Buy a food or spice that you've never tried before. Make a new recipe. Listen to language tapes simply to hear new words. Take a community education class. Read a book on a subject that interests you. Join a hiking group. Volunteer for a group and meet new people. Sit in new places.

As you expand your world, however, make sure that you are not complicating your life. If taking a community education class means that you lose the one evening every week that you have free, then wait until you have more time to take a class. Novelty should be easy and effortless, entering your life freely and blissfully.

Step out of your comfort zone.

Do something new.

3
Addicted to Misery Scoundrel

The Addicted to Misery Scoundrels spend much of their time complaining to themselves or to others. They may be fueled with self-pity and wonder why bad things always seem to happen to them. (This may be coupled with the Negative Thinking Scoundrel.)

They often see themselves as victims rather than the creators of their realities. They blame others for the bad that has happened to them. They may be oblivious to their role in certain situations and relationships.

Because of this characteristic of being "blind" in some way, all addictions are categorized with the Addicted to Misery Scoundrels. Addicts, prior to treatment, are not aware that they have an addiction. (Note: There may be elements of other scoundrels that may be more dominant in a particular person who has an addiction, such as Complacent Scoundrel.)

Because they are comfortable in their gloom, these scoundrels create crazy situations and increase the drama in their lives to maintain a certain level of misery. For instance, they find themselves fifteen minutes early for a meeting, but instead of spending a few minutes preparing for the meeting, they decide to grab a cup of coffee at a nearby coffee shop, where they end up waiting in a long line. Now in a rush, they spill coffee on themselves and sprain their ankle as they dash out the door.

Happiness comes to them through their complaints and the consolation that they receive from their listeners. They may be fortunate in many ways, but these scoundrels seek out ways to focus on tiny negatives in their lives to get their "fix." For instance, they may have a wonderful job, house, marriage and health, but they allow slight signs of aging and a bad friendship to take center stage in their lives. They may well recognize the good in their lives, and yet they speak negatively and seem depressed because of something outside of their control. Even if they begin to look younger in appearance and clear up their friendship, it will be only a short while before Addicted to Misery Scoundrels find something else depressing upon which to dwell.

As parents, they focus on the B+ or A- on an otherwise straight A report card that their child brings home. As homeowners, they notice the spider web in the basement corner. This gives them the appearance of being far from complacent, but Addicted to Misery Scoundrels may not be immediately called to action or desire perfection. They simply need to have something to fuel their misery.

When two or more Addicted to Misery Scoundrels come together, a "pity party" occurs. They connect with others more deeply when both parties can share in their miseries together.

In tense social situations, Addicted to Misery Scoundrels can ease their nerves through their stories of woe, and they may actually be quite entertaining and humorous.

The Addicted to Misery Scoundrels find joy when they are unconsciously engaging in addictive behavior, which includes their addiction to staying unhappy. When they admit they have a problem, they will find joy in overcoming their patterns of addiction and their need to have drama and mishap in their lives. Each time they recognize their craving for gloom, they can switch their focus on making choices that bring peace and simplicity into their lives. Because of the nature of addictive personalities and the downward spiraling effect that can result in their lives, Addicted to Misery Scoundrels can be the most rewarding scoundrel to release.

Comments you might hear from Addicted to Misery Scoundrels:

"You'll never guess what happened to me..."
"Sorry I'm late, but first the dog ran away and then..."
"I am cursed."
"My roof's leaking. My car's in the shop. I think I just broke a crown."
"The reason I'm on crutches is because..."
"Oh sure, the light turns red when I get up to it."
"What's wrong with me? Why don't they like me?"

If you OBSERVE and VERIFY the Addicted to Misery Scoundrel in your life, EXAMINE the following:

1. How has the Addicted to Misery Scoundrel helped you?
2. How has it negatively affected you?
3. To the best of your recollection, when were you first introduced to the Addicted to Misery Scoundrel? Is this a family, cultural or societal scoundrel you consciously or unconsciously accepted as your own?
4. What are some examples of how you've been an Addicted to Misery Scoundrel in the past week?
5. On a scale of one to ten, ten being the best, how would you rate your overall level of satisfaction and happiness in life?
6. In your circle, who else is visited by the Addicted to Misery Scoundrels? Whom do you find yourself complaining to most often?
7. From this moment onward, recognize when you are commiserating with others. Why are you doing it? Have you run out of topics to talk about? Are you nervous? Are you depressed?
8. Make a list of gratitude. Spend at least ten minutes writing everything you appreciate. Keep this list close and revisit it often to deter you from being miserable. It's difficult to see something as bad if you are reminded of twenty or thirty things you love.
9. How can you make your life more ideal? What is one thing you

RELEASE Addicted to Misery Scoundrel Mentality with the following Affirmations:

- ॐ *I have the power to change my reality.*
- ॐ *The Universe supports me when I change my reality for my highest good.*
- ॐ *There are many wonderful things happening in my life and in the world around me.*
- ॐ *I am grateful for all the good in my life.*
- ॐ *I focus on the "good" things in my life.*
- ॐ *When I focus on good, more good comes my way.*
- ॐ *The more good I cast out, the more good I reel in.*
- ॐ *I am assisted by the Universe when I step toward my goals.*
- ॐ *It is not necessary to sacrifice or suffer in order to gain something.*
- ॐ *It is easy and effortless for all of my dreams and desires to be fulfilled.*
- ॐ *My life is easy and fulfilling.*
- ॐ *I choose to create a beautiful reality.*
- ॐ *I am at peace.*
- ॐ *Everything in my life is in good working condition.*
- ॐ *My relationships are nurturing.*

You Are Responsible for Your Happiness

Make a list of things that make you happy. How many of these things can you experience by yourself? If there are very few things on your list that you can do independently, then it's time to discover what things make you happy by yourself.

Many people will say their families are their greatest source of happiness. That is a beautiful thing, but look deeper than that to discover what about your family brings you happiness. Do you enjoy taking care of others? Do you like others taking care of you? Do you like playing games with them? Laughing with them? Sitting quietly in their presence? Do you enjoy the deep soul-to-soul connection with them? Recognize this as a gift, but also recognize that to say you are only happy doing these things with your family is limiting your happiness. It could very well be one source of joy for you, but don't limit yourself to this joy alone.

Remember that you are seeking a life of joy.

That means that you are not looking for a little bit of joy or once-in-a-while joy. You want to find happiness in *everything* you do!

Ideally if something makes you happy, it can be something you share with almost anyone or alone. Choose things that you can do whenever you like and that you can do alone if you choose. Aim to have a good balance of things where you are active and passive so that you have a nice balance of being and doing. For example, singing and listening to music, reading and writing, sitting in nature and gardening.

You may find as you journey on your path that something that once brought you great pleasure no longer does. That is fine. Maybe you need a break for today or forever. You don't need to figure out why it doesn't make you happy anymore. Just do what makes you happy.

Depend upon yourself to be happy. If you want to be happy, discover what you love and what brings you joy and happiness. Fill yourself with that joy and happiness as often as it feels right for you. Expect no one else to make you happy. That expectation leaves you with a chance of happiness and a chance of disappointment. If you want a sandwich, don't sit around and wait for someone to make it for you. It may or may not ever happen. Make your own sandwich.

Be responsible for all of your needs and desires. Just as you do not need to look outside yourself for happiness; you do not need to look outside yourself for a sense of security, for someone to take care of you, for approval, for entertainment, for nurturing or for love. Certainly we can find these things when we are with other people, but we do not need to be dependent on other people for anything. We will avoid disappointment and find contentment within ourselves when we view ourselves as capable and complete.

There certainly can be a great deal of pleasure enjoyed from things outside of ourselves like a beautiful sunset, a kiss, an exquisite meal and a violin concerto, but imagine the amplitude of these pleasures when we are already in a place of joy. Likewise, meeting your soul mate when you are at a place in your life where you are happy and whole allows for a healthy relationship where both of you can grow together and apart in a beautiful rhythm rather than finding constant discord in an unhealthy relationship where two people met under a mutual dependency and are unable to grow separately without increasing that discord.

If you expect your happiness to come from within yourself, you are certain to find happiness. When you are happy with yourself – with who you are and your beliefs, values and ethics, you can be happy simply by being. You no longer need to be doing anything at all. You will find that sitting in the sun can make you happy. Sleeping can make you happy. Breathing can make you happy. For no particular reason at all, you can remain happy every day.

Recognize That You Create Your Reality

Your ability to manifest your reality is easily demonstrated through the very first thing you were involved in – your creation. You began as a single cell and multiplied. You became a baby. You breathed air. You grew. You learned. You became an adult. You have millions of opportunities to choose from every day. Because you were able to come into being, you have already demonstrated that you can create whatever reality you choose. You played a part in the miracle of your birth.

You were the master of your reality. And you have the unlimited resources and ability to manifest your ideal reality today. Every human being has this ability.

So why is it that years, or decades, after birth, we question our ability to manifest the perfect lives for ourselves? Why do we question our connection to God or the Universe? We were nurtured and protected and created in a beautiful image. How can we be so inseparable from our life source for nine months and then, when we fully come into existence, separate ourselves from it?

And then question the separation?

Our creation, gestation and birth show extraordinary faith and trust because there was no other option. We weren't in the womb figuring things out or calculating odds. We were in a constant state of meditation, trusting that our every need would be met. We trusted because there was no other choice and no other way. It was a beautiful trust.

This is what we can have again. Total, complete, unconditional, unwavering trust. Faith. Belief. Conviction. Confidence. Trust.

Why did we lose that unconditional, unwavering trust? How did we go from perfect beings able to manifest all of our needs to being

Addicted to Misery? We are living proof of our unlimited power and yet we simply choose to ignore it. Society has taught us, subconsciously or directly, that we are separate from this power. It teaches us that we must constantly turn to something outside of ourselves for fulfillment, completion and love. Society teaches us that we are not powerful enough as we are now – there is always something missing.

So we begin to search. We don't ask for help from our neighbors because we've learned in our society that we are weak if we ask for help. We try to figure out what it is we need, what is missing from our lives and we spend years, and decades and lifetimes – searching.

We may begin our search with material things. Unfortunately, the reality is that we cannot find lasting contentment in our acquisitions because there is no lasting contentment from external things. We realize this on a soul level, yet we want that happiness, even if it is fleeting. So we continue to buy things and we look to other areas of our lives to fill in the gaps of contentment. We look to our relationships with others, our jobs, our social lives and our religions to find contentment. We may change or modify them in our quest for happiness and we may cling to the qualities we like better in our new choices. We gain happiness.

But it is also ephemeral. Partially this is because we can't remain content for long. It is unfamiliar to Addicted to Misery Scoundrels. We are more familiar with struggle. We do not feel comfortable with our present contentment. For some of us, we are addicted to our drama. We love the rush of adrenaline that flows through us during a time constraint or a challenge. We get scared with too much joy and we somehow manifest a way to sabotage it and return to our familiar pattern of seeking it instead (an aspect of the Fear of Happiness Scoundrel).

Perhaps you or someone you know has questioned if they were where they thought they should be at a certain age based on the parameters of society. This often happens to people in their thirties. They may be single or divorced, feel they are not far enough in their careers, in the right careers or earning big enough salaries; they may worry that their time frame for having children is waning, that they haven't traveled enough or question how they've spent their money.

People in their thirties and forties may hit a "mid-life crisis" because their lives did not turn out as expected and they question what will happen in the future.

The key element that is missing is *trust*. We can trust in our own power to manifest our reality or trust in the power of the Universe to maneuver us safely along our paths. We can trust odds resulting in our favor. We can trust that people have our best interests in mind. We can trust that constant contentment is our birthright, that ultimate joy is attainable. It is within us. It surrounds us. There is no need to search, to acquire or to figure out. It is already there.

It is already here.

We have the power to create our reality. We have the power to manifest all that we need and desire for our highest good. Our thoughts create results in our lives and in the lives of others. We had this power at conception and infancy. And no matter how dormant that power has been, it is still present, its essence always resides within us, no matter what present turmoil we face.

You hold the key that unlocks the vault of joy within *you*. You can release your addiction to misery and your addiction to everything else. You possess never ending, abundant, unconditional joy.

It is already here.

Be at Peace

Creating your reality, living in joy and being at peace are interrelated. When you can fully embrace the truth that you can create your reality, you will see with clarity that you create your happiness and you can therefore live in a state of content. When you are content and you recognize that your needs are met, you will have peace.

The balance of these co-existing states is disrupted, however, when we begin to think and do. We rationalize, argue and get upset. We allow our egos to dominate and become our bosses. We feel separate from each other, from other creatures, from the earth and the Universe. We move from a place of perfect harmony to complete dysfunction through our thoughts. We become powerless, afraid, weak and angry. We move with that bad energy surrounding us in a black cloud and we carry it with us everywhere we go, and spread it to everyone we meet. We move through life with that miserable attitude, compounding it with new experiences that make us more miserable. We resent those who aren't afflicted with their own Addicted to Misery Scoundrels. The longer we do this, the more challenging it is to break free of this destructive cycle.

Stop thinking. Stop doing.

Recalibrate and find peace. It is in the same place it has always been. Inside of you. It may be buried deep, but it is there. Let it surface.

Being at peace allows you to float through your days. Things come to you at the exact right time, in the exact right amount and the exact right way. Everyone and everything in your life is in harmony. It is as though you're leading a magical life, a charmed existence. You remain in a constant state of concord – happy and content. It's as if you're traveling on a road and all the lights are green. Everyone is kind, helping you in every possible way, doling out friendly words and wide smiles.

Being at peace keeps you in an inner state of calm. It's a feeling of being in love, of getting the best job offer you can imagine, of winning the lottery. You are in love with life. You are in love with yourself. Your heart is open and loving. You have love for every creature in the Universe. You express gratitude for all that you have been given and all that is being prepared for you. You trust in the Universe. You release judgment. You can see a positive aspect in everything. You find a lesson in everything that can be perceived as negative. You are in awe of your existence. You are whole and complete. You move with confidence. You manifest all that is for your highest good.

All doubt is shed. All fear is dispersed. All sadness is released. All needs are met. You are wise. You are balanced. You are complete. You are free. You are unique.

You are the one.

You are at peace.

Examine Your Relationships

On a scale of one to ten (ten being outstanding), rate your relationships with the following people:

_____ Your mother
_____ Your father
_____ Your brother(s)
_____ Your sister(s)
_____ Your in-laws and/or step family
_____ Your extended paternal family (aunts, uncles, etc.)
_____ Your extended maternal family
_____ Your significant other
_____ Your daughter(s)
_____ Your son(s)
_____ Your friends
_____ Your boss
_____ Your co-workers/colleagues
_____ Other
_____ Other
_____ Other
_____ Other

Use the spaces labeled "Other" for those who you spend time with or who have a big impact on your life, but are not included on the list. You may want to consider your relationship with a teammate, coach, pastor, doctor, neighbor or roommate. Review your list. Did you record any ones? Twos? How about fives or sixes? What is keeping those relationships from being rated a ten?

Now, take a closer look at the difficult relationships. Do you feel you are being treated unfairly, as though your opinion doesn't matter or you are less intelligent than the other person? Have they said or done anything to you that would prompt you to feel inferior? How did you react to that? Did you stick up for yourself or allow them to dominate the situation?

Often, we treat ourselves more harshly than we would treat others. Sometimes, we allow other people to treat us less than ideally because we have been programmed through our society to accept criticism. Criticism that is delivered with compassion and love is the only acceptable criticism. Criticism that is mean or destructive is unacceptable. People who deliver such criticism do not love themselves. Do not allow yourself to be their scapegoat.

Go back through your list. Are there any other relationships that need to be cleaned up? Is someone gossiping about you? Is someone taking you for granted or not appreciating you? Is there something you have done to someone that you feel guilty about and need to discuss or release?

Addicted to Misery Scoundrels often have some truly miserable relationships. This is okay for them. If they had perfect relationships with everyone, it would be much harder to stay miserable.

If you want to release your scoundrel, however, you've got to free yourself of relationships that aren't serving your highest good. Your happiness will grow as you do this. Pick one person with whom your relationship is less than a ten. Ideally, choose the relationship that would be most helpful to clear. What will it take for this relationship to be a ten or at least higher than it currently is? Come up with one concrete answer and do it.

Let's use the **OVER Technique** with an example of a bad relationship. (The four steps to change are **observe – verify – examine – release**. The **OVER Technique** is described in the Introduction.)

"Tom" took a moment to **observe** all of his important relationships. He rated each relationship and then **verified** that his relationship with his younger sister, Terri, with whom he does not get along, would be the best relationship to heal. Anger was the most expressed emotion in their household and the siblings had been fighting since grade school. Terri lashed out with words, while Tom used his fists. Tom feels that his parents catered more to Terri's needs and that she dominated their attention. It seemed the only way Tom could gain attention was to get into trouble. Now in their thirties, they barely speak to each other, even though they apologized to each other long ago for their mean behavior. Their spouses, children and parents get along well, but feel the tension between Tom and Terri.

As he **examines** this relationship, Tom realizes how he benefits from not healing the relationship with his sister. He doesn't have to face rejection by her if she is not ready to resolve their past. He thinks it is easier not to talk at all rather than make another attempt to get along with her since nothing has worked in the past. He also sees his sister as selfish and different from him in every way. Tom sees no possibility that they could ever have a good relationship.

But let's also examine how Tom is suffering from holding on to this old pattern. He has spent many years with deep resentment and he continues to harbor it toward his sister. This depletes his energy and keeps his heart closed.

The final step is to **release** this negative pattern. In order to release the pattern, Tom must have a *desire* to let it go. If he changes something because he thinks he *should,* the motivation is external rather than internal. Without desire, change becomes difficult and seldom lasts. Tom realizes that he is at a place in his life where he desires resolution with his sister.

To release a pattern, visualize your life after releasing what formerly held you back. Bring this vision to life by sketching or sculpting it so you have a physical representation of what it looks like. In Tom's case, he could draw a picture of himself hugging his sister. Tom visualizes communicating with Terri without getting agitated.

You can write or say positive affirmations to replace your old pattern. To heal his relationship, he affirms to himself: "Everyone in my world only wants what is best for me. My sister only wants what is best for me. I release our past. I release my sister to her highest good and me to mine." There might still be times where Tom gets frustrated when he's around Terri, but he continues to visualize himself being near her without any negative emotional reaction.

When strained relationships between siblings, co-workers, ex-spouses, etc. exist, our two options are to resolve them or break off the relationships. If you're having any negative emotional reaction regarding the other person, like anger or frustration, it's harmful to you. It also allows that person to have power over you. Do you really want the person that you dislike most to dominate your energy field?

There are many cases where it is healthy to free ourselves of relationships with family members that do not suit us. However, in Tom's case, he held resentment and had dissonance around his sister, which affected many people. Any resentment or negative emotional relationships need to be resolved or released. (See Chapter Seven: Stuck in the Past Scoundrel: Eliminate Resentment.) Since Tom is resentful and is sometimes in the same place as his sister, he needs to communicate with her in another attempt to heal their relationship.

If you need to communicate with the other person, perhaps you need to first write a letter to them, so that you can determine exactly what is bothering you. Then take the opportunity to converse. (See Chapter Seven: Stuck in the Past Scoundrel: Release Blame.) If it is appropriate, you can wait until the next time the situation presents itself and then confront the person. For example, if someone calls you stupid when you pronounce a word incorrectly, you can tell them that you don't appreciate being called stupid. Ask for an apology. If the person does not apologize, you can let them know you feel insulted and hurt. End the conversation by walking away from them.

Do not allow yourself to be treated poorly. Do not treat anyone else poorly. Treat yourself as though you are a king or queen. Treat everyone around you with equal dignity and respect. Allow every relationship to be special and enhance your life. You deserve the very best.

Release What Isn't Working

It's easy to leap into joy. You can play your favorite song and be happy. You can get good news, go on a beautiful walk or hold a baby's hand and be elated.

But how long does that feeling last? How long are you able to hold onto blissful experiences before negative energy consumes you?

Many things can bring us instant gratification. But we can easily return to our discontent ten minutes later. Finding happiness in food, drugs, sex and material items can leave us feeling worse than we did earlier. When we look for happiness outside of ourselves, we need to continually get that fix in order to be happy. Our happiness is fleeting because we haven't cleared away the things that weren't working in the first place.

When a car isn't working well, you don't take it to the car wash to make it look prettier. You wouldn't top the tank with gas so that it's nice and full. And you certainly wouldn't buy new floor mats or a new air freshener to make your car feel better. You would fix the car.

That seems obvious. Yet we do similar things in our lives when something isn't working well. We do whatever we can to distract ourselves from whatever isn't right.

That can make us happy for a few hours or a few days, but it will be fleeting until we clear the negative energy in our lives. This includes resolving what isn't working. What we don't want to do is cover this up with a distraction.

What is the first thing you think of when you are asked the following question: What isn't working in your life?

Without giving the question a moment of thought, what answer comes to mind? Your job? A self-sabotaging behavior, such as being late? Your health? A fear of commitment? A fear of failure? A fear of success? Being disorganized? Procrastinating? What is it that you would love to change if only you knew how to change it?

Complete the sentence: "_____ is not working in my life." For example, "My fear of commitment is not working in my life." Say the statement aloud. **Observe** how the statement feels in your body. Do you feel any sensations? Where? In your throat? In your heart? In your lower back? What does it feel like?

After sitting with that observation for a moment, **verify** that this is the greatest issue that isn't working for you right now by asking the question again, "What isn't working in my life?" If the same answer comes, you've found your issue.

Examine how you are benefiting from holding on to this form of self-destruction. We'll use fear of commitment as an example. "Jack" has realized he has a fear of commitment. He feels this in his stomach with a sensation of queasiness. Jack's fear of commitment has kept him moving from place to place his entire adult life. The longest he has ever kept an apartment lease is two years. The longest he has ever kept a job is three years. His longest relationship is nine months. He has lived in six countries and twelve states. He has a background in computer technology, so he is able to contract work for significant amounts of money and take long vacations whenever or wherever he likes. His parents have been married for more than forty years and have been content working together in the same career in the same office for more than twenty years.

How does Jack benefit from his fear of commitment? He never gets bored staying in one place for too long. He doesn't become attached to people or places. He experiences novelty in his life. He travels the world.

After you have recognized the benefits of holding on to what is not working in your life, examine the disadvantages. In Jack's case, his nomadic lifestyle would not need to change at all if there were no disadvantages to his fear. However, he has a few issues he needs to solve. Jack seldom develops long-term relationships, for which he feels he is now ready. He does not know how to deal with conflict resolution. When the going gets tough, Jack has learned that it's time to get going. He has little continuity to his life.

The final step is to **release** this negative pattern. The best way for Jack to release his fear of commitment is to commit to something or someone. He could commit to a job for a few years – maybe one that offers international travel. He could commit to owning real estate, perhaps a house that he can have as a home base which he partially rents to others. He could commit to a relationship – perhaps someone would be willing to travel with Jack around the world. Being that Jack is ready for a long-term relationship, this final option would likely be the best commitment for him to make. He may want to commit to all three options to bring stability into his life, from which a relationship can grow.

A positive affirmation that Jack can use to release his fear of commitment is: *It is safe for me to make a commitment to myself and to other people.* Jack may still need to travel in order to feel safe with his commitments, but he may be able to enjoy weekend outings close to home.

Take a few steps toward changing what isn't working in your life. You may want to go through the **OVER Technique** to help you better understand the reasons why you held on to what hasn't been working for you. Recognizing the advantages and disadvantages of releasing this issue increases the importance of resolution.

There may be some setbacks along the way. Be grateful for them and for what they are showing you. Setbacks are one of the keys to change. Do not get discouraged. Learn from them, release them, and get right back on your path. After all, we wouldn't keep a broken toaster in our kitchen for twenty years, so why should we keep other things in our life that aren't working? Release them and notice how much better life can be.

Release Drama

Addicted to Misery Scoundrels hold tight to their drama, which serves as an addiction. People attract drama into their lives to avoid boredom. They enjoy the thrill of being under time constraints, so they allow barely enough time between appointments or travel destinations. They might be annoyed when they are running late, but they love the rush of adrenaline and the feeling of being slightly pressured and overwhelmed. They love the excitement and uncertainty.

Other examples of drama are: being disorganized, procrastinating, placing impossible tasks upon yourself, setting up insane, extreme challenges like river rafting in bad weather, traveling alone in a dangerous country and associating with notorious people.

The following lists details the differences between drama and excitement:

Drama	Excitement
Tragedy, craziness	*Joy, fun*
High stress level	*Stress is low, living in harmony*
Running late	*Running*
Creating a new tale of woe	*Creating a new painting, song, poem*
Gambling	*Watching a horse race*
Dangerous driving	*Amusement park ride*
Setting ridiculously high expectations	*Setting & meeting an attainable goal*
Making your rent payment a week late	*Making plans for a weekend getaway*

It is great to have a thrilling life, but if the thrills come from drama that carries more stress than fun, it's time to let go of the drama. If you want a peaceful existence, keeping drama around will not help that quest for peace. The two things contradict each other. If you want to live a long and healthy life, you'll need to get rid of stress and the emotional variance that comes with drama.

Observe the dramatic situations in your life. **Verify** them by making a list at the end of every day, entitled: "Ways I Experienced Drama in My Life Today." Any drama, even drama that was not initiated by you, can be written on this list. For instance, if you go for a walk and a dog runs into the road, barking and jumping up on you, this is drama. It was not drama solely initiated by you, unless you were teasing it, but for some reason the dog was drawn to you and you experienced drama because of it. Write it on your list, along with anything that was broken in your presence or didn't work properly, any time you bumped into something, any crazy situation you were in, any odd or heated conversation, any dissonance, any tragedy or conundrum.

Review the list. **Examine** reasons for each dramatic event. Is there any other way you can bring excitement into your life without making it stressful or crazy?

Release real drama by giving up crazy relationships, situations, adventures and schedules. Real drama can be replaced by dramatic entertainment, such as books, movies and plays or board games with imaginary high stakes. You can play or watch sports. You can go for an exhilarating bike ride or hike. You can also find a great deal of excitement by stepping outside of your comfort zone. Sing in public. Give a speech. Take a class in something you want to learn more about.

It would also be a good idea to remember how enjoyable it is to be peaceful and still, not doing anything. Be as lazy as you can for an entire weekend. See how long you can stay in bed and not do anything, not even read. Embrace the simplicity and ease of being. Find excitement in it. Being alive is actually the most exciting thing you'll ever do. Experience that and let go of the craziness.

Release the Need to Emote

One of the many fixations that Addicted to Misery Scoundrels face is getting consumed by their emotions to the point that they are ineffective and unable to function. Six common emotions are detailed below.

Emotion: Sorrow   *Expression: "I'm depressed."*

Although it is not acceptable in many societies to express sadness, it remains highly evident. It is unlikely that anyone will see or hear a grown male crying. It is very likely, however, that we will see advertisements for antidepressants or hear about people who are on them. Sadness is also indirectly expressed in obvious ways that show how it is repressed. People overeat, overwork, under sleep, over sleep and over exercise to fill a void of sadness. People also self-medicate with drugs, alcohol, food, sex or gambling.

Emotion: Fear   *Expression: "I can't."*

Again, this is not an emotion that is typically allowed in Western culture, especially for men. Fear also needs to be repressed. It will express itself as anxiety, violence, rape, erectile dysfunction, frigidity, power struggles and manipulation. Fear can be seen in thought, word and action. Fear can easily be hidden by setting impossible parameters to make it so that you can't possibly begin what it is you're afraid of in the first place. Fear of success and fear of failure are two fears from which thousands of tiny fears are born.

Doubt and anxiety come from a fear that something will not be okay. We may worry about time constraints, money, approval from others and a myriad of other things. Trust that everything happens in its exact time and way.

Aggression is also fear-based. We fear that we will not get our share, our chance, our space, our turn or whatever it is we are seeking. We therefore feel the need to become aggressive to be sure to get what we need and want. If we instead build our level of trust that we are cared for and protected by the Universe, we can release our aggressive nature.

Doubt, anxiety, aggression and fear give away your power. They are wasted emotions.

Emotion: Guilt   Expression: "I'm sorry."

Presented to us through religion, history and ancestry, guilt helps many of our scoundrels stay in control by the premise that we are bad and we don't deserve to be happy. Guilt is most commonly seen by our need to apologize for everything we think, say and do and to apologize for all the things we didn't do, didn't remember, didn't hear, didn't learn and didn't like. We apologize for work we present, speeches we make, food we cook and time we take. Before a speech: "I was up all night with a screaming baby, so bear with me..." Before a meal: "This is a new recipe. I'm not sure how this will taste." Before an idea: "This is a totally new concept, please be open-minded." The list of apologies is long. People are ultimately apologizing for their existence.

Guilt also helps us to take things personally (Chapter Seven: Stuck in the Past Scoundrel: Don't Take Things Personally). We blame ourselves for people's reactions and bad situations.

Guilt and shame appear when we feel we acted wrongly in some manner. We fear we did not live up to our own expectations or the expectations of other people. Believing we are inherently good and forgiving ourselves for past mistakes will release guilt and shame.

Emotion: Anger   Expression: *"Damn it!"*

Anger can be expressed in Western society. In fact, we can be angry most of our lives and be quite powerful, successful people. We can get what we want, especially from people who harbor a great deal of fear, guilt and self-pity. Although it is not acceptable, it is not uncommon for angry people to take out their rage on children, women, pets, customer service representatives, other car drivers and "competitors." Heartburn, heart attacks, high blood pressure, ulcers and strokes can result from angry dispositions. Anger can greatly affect quality and longevity of life.

Anger stems from the belief that our boundaries have been crossed. We become angry toward someone who has wronged us in some way. We may be angry at ourselves as well. We could be angry at our bosses for making us work long hours or giving us tasks we dislike. We may be angry at our spouses for ignoring our needs. We may become angry at our children for not listening to us.Someone has violated our sense of what is right or fair. Sometimes, we are not conscious of our boundaries being crossed. Other times, we are afraid to communicate. We bypass expressing our desires rationally because of an unconscious fear that we will not receive what we need and we become angry.

Emotion: Self-Pity   Expression: *"There's something wrong with me."*

This emotion is highly expressed by Addicted to Misery Scoundrels. "Poor me" is a common mantra unconsciously guiding people with a great deal of self-pity. The underlying fear is that of being unlovable. Because of this, they are attracting people and situations to their lives that continue to perpetuate unhappiness. Those who operate from a place of self-pity manifest problems to gain negative attention, such as being tired, sick, poor, hungry, too hot or too cold. Nothing is ever quite right for the person with self-pity.

In society, we hear self-pity expressed subtly, but often: "This is hard." "Life is hard." "This is killing me." "I'm tired."

Addictions of any kind falsely soothe self-pity.

Emotion: Envy   Expression: "I want that."

We look to those who seem happy to see what it is they have that we do not. What we usually see is the external picture, rather than the internal truth. There is no amount of material goods or money that will ever make us happy. There is no amount of substances that will ever make us happy. There is no exact job, partner, home, pet or town that will make us happy. Happiness is internal. It has absolutely *nothing* to do with *anyone else*. Through self-love and self-approval we gain happiness.

Being jealous of other people's lifestyles (Grass is Greener Scoundrel) does not express our compassion or joy toward them. Instead it shows resentment toward them and internal resentment that we are not living the way we want to be. We fear that an aspect of our lives is lacking. Affirm to yourself: *I am enough. I have enough.* Be grateful for all you have. Slowly change what isn't working for you and be ready to receive all that is for your highest good.

The desire we have to drown in these emotions and vacillate between emotional extremes is an addiction that needs to be released. Addicted to Misery Scoundrels (and most other) scoundrels share a common need to wallow in a life of unhappiness. If you want to live a life of ultimate joy, move to a place of emotional stability. In any situation that triggers you emotionally, use the energy of that emotion to your benefit by playing that emotion like the winning card in poker. If that emotion is going to weaken your spirit, leaving you depressed and non-functioning, then take a deep breath and wait to react. You'd be better off processing that emotion later. Keep your poker face and deal with the situation at hand effectively.

This does not mean you will be suppressing words or emotions. On the contrary, releasing the need to emote gives you permission to move beyond primal, spontaneous reactions toward integration of thoughtful measured responses and diplomacy. It frees the need to get caught up in the emotional turmoil into which many people have been programmed. It clears the dependency and comfort of familiar negative emotions, so that you do not get consumed by the emotion.

Let's take a look at a few examples to fully explain the difference between using emotions effectively and drowning in emotional turmoil.

- You get lost while driving and get angry.
- Your neighbors throw garbage in your yard and you are angry.
- You plan an event and only three people show up, making you sad and angry.

In the first scenario, your anger is a wasted emotion. Recalibrate your route so that you can arrive as smoothly and effectively as possible. Next time, get clearer directions and verify them with a second source.

In the second situation, use your anger to your advantage. Communicate with your neighbors in a calm, but firm manner. Help them realize that you are aware that they threw garbage in your yard and you do not appreciate it. Ask them to clean it up.

In the third instance, you can benefit from your sadness and anger. It seems that it's unfortunate that only three people came to your event, but it may be those were the exact three people that needed to be there with you. Be grateful to them for coming and make sure none of your anger or sadness is reflected toward them. Examine why you are angry and sad. Likely, it's because you feel like a failure, you feel unlovable, unimportant and unworthy of people's time.

Use this information to your advantage. How? If you plan on organizing anything in the future, determine what went wrong this time. Was there enough time to plan the event? Was it a good day or time? Did you remind people of the event? Did you have an invitation? Did you personally inform people of the event and let them know how important their presence is? Did you have any negative thoughts or doubts that may have energetically altered the attendance?

Your sadness and anger are letting you know you are unhappy with someone or something. Respect your emotions. Don't sink into them; use them to prod you in the right direction. For instance, do not ride an emotional roller coaster when you learn that your most successful friend got a promotion that triples her salary while you are barely able to pay your rent. Recognize the feelings that arise: anger (that she got a promotion), jealousy (that she is wealthy and you aren't), sorrow (that you feel jealous), self-pity (that you aren't wealthy), guilt (that you should make more money than you do) and fear (that you will never make a decent salary). Use those emotions to determine what job you would really love to do and get creative on how to make a great salary doing it. Harness positive energy toward creating the perfect, lucrative dream job and take steps toward manifesting that job into reality.

Your happiness is dependent upon dealing with your emotions effectively. Positive thinking combined with effective emotion and appropriate action will attract all you need and desire.

All of these negative emotions come from a place of fear (See Chapter Four: Fear of Happiness Scoundrel: Release Your Fear.). They arise from the ego. The ego thrives on the belief that it, and you, are separate from the rest of the Universe. In truth, you and the Universe are one.

Negative emotions are powerless in the presence of love. Love is the opposite emotion of fear. Unconditional love, self-approval and acknowledgement of a continuous universal connection will obliterate the ego, and the negative emotions of sadness, fear, guilt, anger, self-pity and jealousy. When you love and approve of yourself no matter what situation you face, you maintain a beautiful level of calm. This is an important key to living in joy.

Release All Addictions from Your Life

An addiction is a dependency on something, such as drugs, gambling, work, sex, exercise, a relationship, a routine, an emotion (misery, anxiety, guilt), food restriction or binge eating. Addictions are created in an attempt to deal with pain, especially pain from childhood. The core negative belief, *I'm not good enough*, often lurks in the addict's subconscious.

Addicts are unable to stop indulging in their addictions. They become anxious or irritable when they are away from their addictions for too long. Stress, disappointments and depression can trigger the need for a "fix," which will result in temporary relief. However, after the fix, intense shame and guilt surface leading to more pain and eventually another fix.

This cycle can be broken when addicts accept their problems and realize they are controlled by their addictions. To end the addiction, implement many of the same suggestions offered in Chapter One: Complacent Scoundrel: Exercise. Make sure you have a true desire to change. It is also important to have a good support network. Friends, family and professionals can rally together to help you through your addiction. A program, such as a twelve step program or hypnotherapy, which specializes in conquering addictions, can be helpful. Frequent rewards can be a great external motivator to keep you on track. When you face a setback, do not allow guilt or shame to overtake you. Return to your program and focus on the positive changes that you've made.

In addition to the suggestions in Chapter One, you can also add a positive replacement for the empty space left by the addiction, such as exercising or reading. You may initially want to have a complete change of atmosphere for the first few weeks to break the former routine and psychological "habit" of the addiction. Keep yourself focused on the present moment through deep breathing, meditation and journaling to avoid feelings of being overwhelmed about the future. Use the power of the elements and the natural balance of bio-rhythms. Get plenty of sleep, spend time in nature, enjoy long baths, sit by a fire, eat healthy food, drink water and laugh.

Addictions stem from the desire to relieve pain, but the unfortunate irony is that they only cause more pain for the addict because of the negative consequences that result from addictions. In order to live a life of joy, we obviously need to be free from pain. We also need to be free from a dependency on fleeting external sources of happiness. Breaking free from all negative thoughts, both conscious and unconscious, help us to let go of unhealthy relationships, situations, emotions and addictions. Being centered, grounded and self-assured catapults your life from a place of dysfunction to a place of harmony. From here, there is no need to depend on anything. From this place, you maintain an existence of complete trust in the Universe. You know, without a speck of doubt, that your needs are met. The external search, along with all addictions, ends with this trust.

4
Fear of Happiness
Scoundrel

Fear of Happiness Scoundrels believe that life is precipitously balanced between happiness and sadness. When they allow themselves to be in total bliss, they get nervous and await the certain tragedy that they believe will arise at any moment. They believe in an equilibrium of happiness and sadness in life.

Many Fear of Happiness Scoundrels and/or their parents have been raised in a religious setting. The fire and brimstone mentality of several religions suggests that humans were born of evil and sin is inevitable. Fear of going to hell and eternal sorrow keep these scoundrels in line. Many people associate joy and happiness with things that are "sinful," such as sex, drugs, rock and roll, dancing, movies and chocolate cake. We have learned to create guilt and shame around many of these pleasures. Instead of focusing on the total bliss obtained from our pleasures, we focus on suppressing the hypothetical negative consequences from our actions. It becomes much more difficult to enjoy chocolate cake when we believe we'll get fat from it.

In order for Fear of Happiness Scoundrels to be able to indulge without much or any guilt or shame, they must justify the reason behind the indulgence. Chocolate cake served in celebration of a birthday becomes a necessary ritual in which we must partake in order to honor the person's birthday. Indulging in healthy pleasures without the need to justify them can be highly beneficial for these scoundrels.

Often it feels better and safer for Fear of Happiness Scoundrels to be stuck in unhappiness because they are comfortable with their known unhappiness. The imaginary unhappiness that may be lurking around the corner is what they want to avoid and the best way to do that is stay away from living a life steeped in happiness and "guilty" pleasures.

Happiness therefore comes to these scoundrels when they are only moderately happy because they are expecting only moderate unhappiness around the next corner. Joy can be found for Fear of Happiness Scoundrels when they seek contentment. If the fire and brimstone mentality exists for them, the mentality can be released by trusting in the knowledge that we are made in the image of the divine and we are meant to be living a life of joy.

Comments you might hear from Fear of Happiness Scoundrels:

"Everything's going so well in my life. I'd better not push my luck."
"I know this is horrible for me, but I'll just have one tiny scoop, please."
"Paris is romantic, but maybe we should visit New Hampshire instead. It would be a more sensible trip."
"I think we'd better call it an evening before we explode from having too much fun."
"This is so good it's got to be a sin!"

If you OBSERVE and VERIFY the Fear of Happiness Scoundrel in your life, EXAMINE the following:

1. How has the Fear of Happiness Scoundrel helped you?
2. How has it negatively affected you?
3. To the best of your recollection, when were you first introduced to the Fear of Happiness Scoundrel? Is this a family, cultural or societal scoundrel you consciously or unconsciously accepted as your own?
4. What are some examples of how you've been a Fear of Happiness Scoundrel in the past week?

5. On a scale of one to ten, ten being the best, how would you rate your overall level of satisfaction and happiness in life?
6. In your circle, who else is visited by the Fear of Happiness Scoundrels? Are there ways you enable each other to avoid happiness?
7. From this moment onward, recognize when you are afraid of happiness. Why are you afraid?
8. What negative consequences have you experienced from having too much fun? Are these memories serving as reminders for you to limit your happiness now? Is it realistic to think that these consequences will revisit you?
9. How can you make your life more ideal? What is one thing you can do TODAY?

RELEASE Fear of Happiness Scoundrel Mentality with the following Affirmations:

- ॐ *I welcome new people and situations into my life with joy and trust.*
- ॐ *Releasing all fear allows the Universe's divine plan to manifest.*
- ॐ *I embrace the unknown of the future.*
- ॐ *It is easy and safe to be happy.*
- ॐ *Joy is abundant for me in the present moment.*
- ॐ *I bask in the safety of my own happiness.*
- ॐ *I deserve love and joy.*
- ॐ *I deserve to indulge in the abundance of the Universe.*
- ॐ *It is safe to open my heart.*
- ॐ *I am happy and whole.*

Release Your Fear

Feelings stem from two basic emotions, fear and love. Guilt, shame, anger, doubt, anxiety, impatience, jealousy, aggression, resentment, depression and many other emotions grow from fear (See also Chapter Three: Addicted to Misery Scoundrel: Release the Need to Emote). They come from the beliefs that we are not good enough, we will not get our fair share, we are unlovable, we are unworthy, we do not have enough and we do not do enough. They come from a fear that we are not safe and protected in the Universe and we are not one with the Universe. They come when we blindly and stubbornly impose our will against our intuition and divine plan.

Fear is driven by ego. It keeps us divided and alone. We are left to "figure out" rather than allow our path to unfold. Harboring fear of any type separates us from our source of wisdom, life, power and ability. It freezes us. Fear shows us that we doubt ourselves and our talents, as well as our ability to trust in the Universe. Fear also focuses our energy on exactly what it is we fear.

"Christine" experienced a moment of great fear walking alone late at night while living in a foreign country. Available taxi drivers honked at her, beckoning her to ride with them. Wanting only to stretch her legs and breathe fresh autumn air, Christine ignored the taxis. But soon enough, her fears played on her and she realized she shouldn't be walking alone at night in a strange city. Frightened, she decided to take the next taxi.

Within a few seconds, a mini-van taxi slowed beside her on the road. The driver offered her a ride even though it was after his normal working hours. She accepted. Five minutes later, the driver had parked the van against a brick wall in a dark alley. Christine was certain he would rape her. She screamed and kicked at the door as he approached her. Realizing she was going to fight, the driver changed his mind and retreated, drove to the main road and kicked her out of the van. She ran the rest of the way home.

Christine had been safe until she became afraid and changed her course of action. Her fear of being raped had nearly manifested itself.

Fear limits us and keeps us in a state of withholding all that is for our highest good. Giving power to our fear sends a message to the Universe that we believe in the possibility that bad things can happen to us.

We may have been hurt in the past and therefore become more limiting with ourselves and others to avoid further pain. For protection, we may shut down or isolate ourselves. However, this will only serve to keep away the good the Universe has to offer us.

Going to an interview, you can either believe you will get the job or you won't. Which attitude is more likely to get us hired? The fearful, pessimistic energy you are releasing from your belief that you will not get the job, or even that you *may* not get the job, will not benefit you in any manner. The employer will sense that energy and will accommodate your belief by not hiring you. You are much better off believing you will get the job even if you have absolutely none of the necessary skills. It's not up to you to decide if you should be hired or not. Leave it to the hiring team and to the Universe. If you are meant to be working there, you will get the job. The "skills" they may need in that environment might be completely different than what was initially stated. Do not lie about your skills. But do not decide for a company that you are not the right employee for them if you want to be working there.

In this case, and in many others, fear keeps us from reaching our dreams. It must retreat in order for us to be fulfilled.

What are you afraid of? Some common fears are: growing old, getting cancer, losing people close to you, being financially stable and independent, death, war, rape, fire, flood, famine, getting fat, being unable to afford good medical care, never getting married, never having children, your children failing, losing your memory, losing your mind, never getting organized, never catching up, the car breaking down and public speaking.

The list can go on and on. Let it. Write down every fear you have ever had. Begin with childhood fears, whether they have been resolved or not. Write about adolescent fears that manifest when you're with your colleagues. Write down your mother's and father's fears that they have passed on to you.

Look at your complete list. What fears are irrational? What fears come from other people? Did you have a friend growing up that worried about getting cancer and therefore you worried, too?

Identifying your fears is the first part of releasing them. After you have written your list of fears, write a second list of positive affirmations. For example, if you are afraid of getting cancer, you can affirm to yourself: "I make healthy choices. Everything I do brings me closer to living a healthier, more fulfilling life." Of course, saying and writing these affirmations without acting upon them is only completing half the job. If you put carcinogens in your body, you are not making healthy choices. If your mind knows that, then so does your body. Acting against your affirmations is counterproductive. Instead, take action toward making them your new reality.

Releasing your fear will reconnect you to your source of everything. Letting go of your trepidation in life will allow you to reclaim power and happiness.

Find Joy in Daily Activities

There are daily activities that simply need to get done – cooking, cleaning, laundry, yard work, driving, brushing our teeth, getting dressed and paying bills. How are we supposed to find joy among these things?

First of all, understand that some people do find great joy in all of these things, some people find joy in a few of them and some people, especially Fear of Happiness Scoundrels, find joy in none of them. More than anything, your state of mind will determine the pleasure in any activity. If you're a happy person, then you're a happy person brushing your teeth, you're a happy person driving your car and you're a happy person sweeping the floor.

The rationale behind having no joy in your daily activities, is that it will leave a possibility to experience joy in bigger and better things. Fear of Happiness Scoundrels believe there is a finite amount of joy that can occur before negative consequences arise. If you are too happy sweeping the floor and brushing your teeth, you'll steal joy away from watching a movie or playing cards.

Even though it's easy to become joyful, there may still be some activities that you really dislike or are indifferent to doing. You can't imagine *ever* being joyful while doing these activities. How can you change this?

Use the same four suggestions given in Chapter One: Complacent Scoundrel: Exercise:

- Visualize yourself doing the activity with joy.
- Add in a joyful component to the activity.
- Make a conscious choice to be happy.
- Reward yourself with something that makes you joyful.

First of all, visualize yourself doing the activity with a smile on your face. Perhaps you're even humming, whistling or singing. Visualize the activity being simple and easy for you. Visualize it going smoothly. Visualize yourself getting help if you need it. Visualize yourself after the task is done. You feel good about yourself and relieved that you have accomplished the task that you have formerly disliked. Go through this visualization exercise every time you need to until you find joy in the activity.

For example, let's say you dislike driving on the highway. You become anxious at the thought of it. Turning onto the entrance ramp, your palms sweat as you grip the steering wheel tightly, creating tension in your hands, especially your knuckles, wrists and forearms. Your shoulders elevate and hunch forward, your jaw clenches, stress accumulates in your face, your eyes and between your eyebrows. Your blood pressure rises. Your heart rate increases. You turn into a mass of distress.

You worry that you won't merge into the flow of traffic easily, because there have been times in the past that you haven't. There always seems to be a string of cars in the slow lane and none of them let you merge. When you finally manage to get on the highway, people aggressively cut you off. Other drivers tailgate behind you, urging you to go faster. You check and double check every exit sign, certain you missed your exit. You call to verify the directions, nearly swerving into another lane and then almost miss your exit. You have to slam on your brakes to exit.

Wow! Replaying that scenario in your mind would be enough to keep anyone from wanting to drive on the highway.

Visualizing the same activity with joy, however, is quite different. This time, be confident in your abilities as you enter the highway. Your palms are dry, you hold the steering wheel capably. Your body is relaxed and comfortable. Your jaw is slack, your eyes are relaxed, your shoulders are retracted and depressed, your heart rate and blood pressure remain level. You are joyful and grateful. With few cars around you, you enter the flow of traffic with ease. Other cars around you on the road drive a safe distance from you, respecting your space. Directions are easy for you to follow. You always have advanced warning that your exit is coming. Exiting the highway is effortless. You arrive at your destination invigorated and happy. You reward yourself by listening to your favorite song, which makes you even happier.

The two scenarios are completely different and visualizing one versus the other could result in two completely different outcomes. Even if what you visualize does not happen as you foresaw it, you are still left with an edgy feeling from the first visualization and a peaceful feeling from the second.

Athletes use visualization techniques before their performances. They see themselves executing their talents with precision which results in their success. They add in a joyful component, which can be as simple as the pleasure they feel from moving their bodies with the strength and flexibility they have cultivated throughout the years. The joy they experience is easily witnessed through the passion they exhibit in their performances. Their reward is intrinsic, knowing they have done their best, and extrinsic, through their medals and accolades.

Just like athletes, you can add in a joyful component, which may need to be external at first. This could be as simple as playing upbeat music or inviting a friend to entertain you while you complete your task.

You can also reward yourself when a task is completed. Keep your rewards for daily activities simple. Perhaps you take a short nap after taking out the garbage or call your best friend after washing the dishes. More then anything, find gratitude in your ability and opportunity to do any activity. View tasks as privileges rather than forced necessities. Move with an energy of peace, calm and joy.

Open Your Heart

Many Fear of Happiness Scoundrels operate from the head, carefully thinking, weighing the pros and cons and making decisions that make sense based on the current situation. You may have a choice on Sunday night to prepare for a Monday morning presentation or to watch a movie. Your heart may beg you for the relaxing, enjoyable entertainment, but your mind tells you to run through that presentation one more time. Remembering how you already indulged in a night on the town Friday and played golf on Saturday, you decide that enough fun was had and now it is time to focus on work again.

Seems like a fairly logical choice, even though you spent the past two weeks working on the presentation and five hours Saturday night perfecting it. But wouldn't it help you to review your material one more time?

Perhaps not.

Perhaps having a little less polished speech will make your endorphins flow and make your speech more passionate. It may make your words more genuine and less rehearsed. You could also seem more approachable for questions and suggestions. And perhaps watching the movie will inspire you in some way that will further enhance your presentation.

So what is the better choice?

Ask your heart.

Sometimes the practical choice is not the better choice. The better choice is the one that comes from the heart. Fear of Happiness Scoundrels often think that too much fun and not enough work are the ingredients for failure. Often times, however, it is the exact opposite: the greatest successes come when we honor our heart and follow our passion.

In many cases, Fear of Happiness Scoundrels would be better off going with the option that is more fun, even if their minds tell them differently. The best solution in any decision-making process is to check in with your heart and your intuition.

From a physical perspective, allow your body to move in ways that keep your heart open. Remind yourself to keep your arms at your sides rather than crossing them over your chest. Relax your shoulders away from your ears. Stand tall with your chest lifted and open. Do not hunch your back or hide behind things. Wear green, the color of the heart chakra. Do a small back bend from time to time to bring awareness into your chest and energy into your body. Stretch your arms wide, releasing that heart energy into your arms, hands and fingers. They are extensions of the heart and provide us numerous ways to connect with others.

Respect your heart. Listen to it. Open it. Allow yourself to be vulnerable. And trust that you are safe within your vulnerability.

Allow yourself to be wide open to everything that is for your highest good. So often we stay stuck in our comfort zones, in our tiny self-constructed and self-perceived boxes. We tend to include people in our lives whom we think share our same interests, beliefs, status and background. These choices may be based on the ego and they can keep us from opening our hearts. Of course, when you feel that someone or something is wrong for you, it is beneficial to release that person or thing. But when everything feels right and good, be open to receiving all the abundance, happiness and beauty the Universe has to offer.

Allow that abundance to come into your life in every way. Open your heart to the earth, the wind, the sky and the ocean. Open your heart to plants and animals living in harmony. Open your heart to those who love you. Open your heart like an innocent, trusting child. Open it as though you have never been hurt in your life. Trust that the Universe will expose you to what is for your highest good.

Be open to the happiness that is your birthright. Fear nothing — especially do not fear your own happiness. Open your heart and your soul. See yourself in others. See others within yourself. The only separation that exists is within our minds. Allow that separation to diminish. Allow your walls to retreat. Live your life with abandon. Trust that the world is filled with love and compassion. Add to that depth of love. Jump into it. Dive into it. Belly flop and somer-sault into it. Let all the love in the world fill your heart and your soul. And let that love cascade from every breath you breathe, every thought you think and every action you take.

Smile

Feeling unhappy? Coax a smile out of yourself. Show your teeth. Keep that smile for at least sixty seconds. It's possible that at the end of sixty seconds, your mood will remain gloomy, but odds are you'll be more joyful. Even focusing on the picture of a smile is uplifting. The upturned corners of the lips on a smile help to elevate moods.

Smiling also gets you into "the zone." It makes your personal magnetism soar. You harness more positive energy. You are more approachable with a smile on your face. Smiles, like yawns, are also "contagious" and highly reciprocal.

Sometimes you may be in a rotten mood and you force yourself to smile and it only makes you more miserable. Those are the times when apple pie and balloons probably wouldn't shift your mood one tiny bit. A fake smile won't make a difference either.

You can stubbornly make sure it won't.

But how much stubbornness does it take to keep you in a bad mood? How much energy is required to keep you feeling rotten? Quite a lot, especially if you are dragging your feet or moving with aggression, protecting yourself from the world around you. The problem with being melancholy is that you aren't aware how difficult it can be.

Being happy is much easier. For the rest of the week, your top priority is to smile. Whenever you're conscious of not smiling, smile. Feel it light up your face and the energy around you. Feel tension fade in your facial muscles.

Smile at yourself. Smile at others. Smile at the sun, the flowers, children, dogs, and dragonflies. Smile with sincerity. Look people in the eye. Say hello if you choose. Be confident in yourself even if the other person or creature doesn't respond or responds negatively. Simply release the interaction and keep on smiling.

Nurture Yourself with Luxury

Attention, Fear of Happiness Scoundrels – it's time to indulge!

In order to release this scoundrel, you must pamper yourself. You deserve something that makes you feel luxurious and special. It need not be an expensive thing, only something in which you would not normally indulge. Buy fresh raspberries or fresh flowers. Treat yourself to a fancy Japanese dinner or to the symphony. Buy an exquisite bubble bath gel and take a long, candlelit bath. Sip champagne under the stars. Get a massage or a new pair of shoes. Pick out a pastry at the best bakery in town. Take a day off work and get a pedicure. Or do all of the above. Whatever you choose, make sure it screams luxury for you.

Years ago, I went shopping for a few necessary items for winter. I had found a sweater, but what I really wanted was a new winter coat. I debated even looking at winter coats because I had a perfectly good one in my closet, at least it was perfectly good nine years ago.

So, I peeked at the coats. Among the coat racks was a fake purple leopard print fur coat. It was extremely unique and sparked my interest. I tried it on and instantly fell in love with it, but wondered if it was something that I could "pull off." Did my personality say purple leopard print fur coat? I returned the coat back to its hanger and walked to the cash registers with my sweater. But upon waiting in line for a moment, I turned around and retrieved the coat.

For the next five months, whenever I wore my crazy purple coat, I felt luxurious. Eventually, I had a matching purple purse and hat. I've received more compliments on that coat than on any item of clothing – all for the price of forty-six dollars.

What is it that would make you feel luxurious? If you can't think of anything and you don't often go shopping, maybe it's time to go. Go window shopping until something strikes your fancy. It may appeal to your sight, sound, touch, taste or smell or perhaps it appeals to all your senses. Remember, it doesn't have to be expensive, but it does have to be luxurious. Buy it without guilt. Buy it because you deserve to be pampered.

Recognize that this is not an attempt to buy happiness. This is an assignment to *indulge*. It is an assignment to release your block against happiness. Whatever you choose, savor your indulgence with all the pleasure *you* deserve.

Be certain you partake in the indulgence by yourself first, and then with someone else later, if you choose. By indulging alone, you are focusing entirely on *your* pleasure and no one else's pleasure. You are also indulging strictly to indulge. Don't attempt to indulge with any justification. For instance, don't buy fresh berries to make your sister a pie to celebrate her new house. Buy the berries to make *yourself* a pie and celebrate yourself as you indulge in a healthy serving of pie. Later, share the pie with your sister or enjoy it by yourself or with friends and family throughout the week.

While you are indulging in whatever way you choose, release any negative thoughts that come up, such as: *I shouldn't be doing this. This is ridiculous. This can't be good for me. I'll have to say a few rosaries after this.* Continually remind yourself as you indulge: I deserve to indulge in the abundance of the Universe.

Never Ending Vacation

Think about the joy and excitement you feel on vacation. After you've settled at your destination, you take a deep breath and stretch your arms wide. You're grateful that you arrived safely, that you're in a beautiful new atmosphere with friends, family or with the fantastic opportunity to vacation by yourself and meet other travelers and locals. You're open to the exciting experiences that await you. Every day presents you with opportunities to play. You're in a completely different state of mind than you are at home. This allows for more freedom of thought, more creativity, less inhibition, less logical thinking, less worry and more spontaneous decisions fueled by your desires.

Travel back in time to your last vacation. Notice what you did differently while you were on vacation from what you do in your normal day-to-day life. Did you go to sleep later to enjoy the night life and wake up later than usual? Or did you get to bed earlier and wake up earlier, eager to greet the day? How are your biorhythms different than they are at home? Do you have more energy? Are you more willing to initiate conversations with strangers? Are you more generous? Is your heart more open? Do you feel moments of ultimate joy and perfection?

Let that carefree bliss of vacation flow into your everyday life. Weekly "vacations" help tremendously. Schedule vacation time with yourself. It could be the same time every week, or a fluctuating vacation time. Just be sure it gets scheduled. Also, make sure that you block at least four hours for your mini-vacation. In any given week, you have one hundred and sixty-eight hours. That gives you forty-two potential vacation blocks. With forty-two available options, there is no excuse not to book your vacation every week.

If possible, turn that four-hour vacation into an entire day. Make it a Sabbath day for yourself, where you do no work at all. If you have a flexible work week, Wednesdays are a nice day to have to yourself because they are the perfect midpoint to the week and because most people are at work, therefore you can really keep this day to yourself. If you work regular business hours, Saturdays or Sundays are the more traditional days to rest. They are well-earned and much needed.

On your Sabbath, feel free to do whatever makes you totally happy and alive. Stay in your pajamas all day. Eat whatever you like or spend the day fasting with the elements. Ideally, spend the day at home. Your Sabbath day is a great day to be with your family or friends or to simply be by yourself. Make sure that everything you do on your Sabbath is what you truly want to be doing. Ask yourself before any activity if that is how you really want to spend your day. If cleaning the bathtub is not on your list of things you would really enjoy that day, wait until the next day. If you would enjoy doing laundry and dishes on your Sabbath, then do them. If not, it won't be the worst thing in the world to procrastinate for a day. Check in with your heart and follow its direction.

The less mental and physical energy you expend on your Sabbath the more enthusiasm you have to do mental and physical tasks on the other six days of the week. Allow yourself a day to relax and goof off.

If a weekly vacation day is impossible, stick to a four-hour vacation. It's a great option when you're sneaking in too much productivity on your Sabbath day. Better to fully indulge in a four-hour vacation than halfway indulge in a twenty-four-hour one.

Be careful not to sacrifice your vacation to friend or family obligations (Martyr Scoundrels). If you can, put money toward your vacation to solidify it in your calendar. Keeping it at the same time every week will also help you be loyal to your vacation.

On your vacation, be a tourist in your world. Make plans with someone or go solo to an exciting spot you love or have always wanted to see. Get dressed up or wear your most comfortable, casual clothes that you love. Visit a nice restaurant on your vacation, or cook a meal at home, consciously creating it with love and health. Pick a new spot each week to visit as if you were a tourist. Go to an art museum, the symphony, a park or a theatre. Buy yourself a treat on vacation; be generous with others, outgoing, carefree, less inhibited, more playful, more spontaneous and more indulgent.

Carry that feeling of a never ending vacation throughout your week. Bliss is available to you day after day because you are a kind and good person. There is nothing to fear. And no repercussions will follow. Live as though you are on a never ending vacation. Because the best vacations are the ones that put you in a beautiful state of excitement and ease and keep you there.

You deserve the very best life has to offer.

The Elements

Earth. Air. Water. Fire. The four elements were the foundation of ancient civilizations and they are still the foundation for most living things. For thousands of years, our ancestors lived in close proximity with the elements. They were in balance and harmony with these elements. Each element is important and has a different influence on us. Each of them has healing properties.

The earth grounds us. It supports us. It supports abundant plant life which provides us food, oxygen and housing. It also sustains animal life. We can choose a "power place" on the earth. This can be a special spot we sit or lie upon each day and access the power of the earth. Activities that tap into the earth's energy include fasting and nourishing our bodies, and getting an appropriate amount of exercise.

The air transports the oxygen, minerals, elements and seeds needed for life. It cools us and warms us. It gives us energy. Breathing and meditating are two ways we can appreciate the element of air.

Water, comprised of hydrogen and oxygen, is integral to life. It is necessary for our bodies to function. Water is symbolic of rebirth and renewal. It is a universal solvent. It is a medium for life. Like land, it supports both plants and animals. Warm water relaxes us. Cool water refreshes us.

Fire gives us warmth, power and energy. As a healing medium, it can rid us of toxins and energy pollution that we absorb from our environment. It opens and balances our energy centers, as does warm water.

In the last century, we have shifted away from the balance that is found in the natural world. We spend less time outdoors and more time with machines – televisions, computers, radios, cars, exercise equipment, boats, motorcycles, airplanes, moving walkways, elevators, trains, buses and golf carts. Many people fail to recognize the healing powers of the elements.

How can we shift our lifestyles so they are more harmonious with nature?

Safely experiment with each of the elements by lying on the earth, sitting alone by a fire, bathing and breathing. Fear of Happiness Scoundrels can learn to indulge in the elements without consequence. They can develop a deeper spiritual connection as adults in the wilderness beyond what they may have learned in their childhood. Witness the ongoing contentment and harmony in the natural world. Other animals live a carefree life, in tune with the elements. We can, too.

Whether you are conscious of their effects or not, the elements are a powerful quartet. Discover which of them brings you into harmony and inspires your creativity during certain seasons or certain months. Tap into the abundant healing energy and power of the elements.

5
Martyr Scoundrel

Martyr Scoundrels put other people before themselves. They are likely to give up their free time or special planned events to help someone else, especially a family member, to whom they have incredible loyalty. They are passive and find it difficult to say no.

Often, their parents were very demanding, controlling, aloof or disapproving. As children, they were unable to gain the approval they wanted from one or more parents or parental figures. As adults, they continue to look to others for approval. Martyr Scoundrels may re-create the same parenting patterns with their children. They also may enact the exact opposite parenting behavior, but with the same end result. For instance, someone raised by a disapproving parent would become an aloof parent. In both cases, the parents never voice their approval.

Many Martyr Scoundrels spend their entire lives striving for perfection in themselves to attain this imaginary approval. They may pass this curse on to their children and their friends. Criticism and gossip result from their high rate of disapproval of others. This quality does not draw people close to them, which will only further push them to perfection and approval seeking.

Martyr Scoundrels are often manipulated by family and close friends. They often marry someone similar to their disapproving parent and raise disapproving children, who reflect their parents' disapproval of them. The unspoken message Martyr Scoundrels send the Universe is: *Other people's needs come before mine.* They become drained and unfulfilled, resentful and unhappy.

Martyr Scoundrels find a great deal of happiness in serving others. This masks their inability to say no and offers them some approval from those they serve. When they recognize someone taking advantage of them and they are still unable to say no, unhappiness results.

Martyr Scoundrels who can find proper balance between their needs and others' needs find balanced happiness.

Comments you might hear from Martyr Scoundrels:

"Sure I can cancel my massage to help you move."
"I can't see that concert with you. I cook my mother dinner every Saturday night."
"Of course you can stay with us for a few months. You can have my bed."
"I'll be glad to do all of Kara's duties while she's on maternity leave."

If you have OBSERVED and VERIFIED the Martyr Scoundrel in your life, EXAMINE the following:

1. How has the Martyr Scoundrel helped you?
2. How has it negatively affected you?
3. To the best of your recollection, when were you first introduced to the Martyr Scoundrel? Is this a family, cultural or societal scoundrel you consciously or unconsciously accepted as your own?
4. What are some examples of how you've been a Martyr Scoundrel in the past week?
5. On a scale of one to ten, ten being the best, how would you rate your overall level of satisfaction and happiness in life?
6. In your circle, who else is visited by the Martyr Scoundrels? What similar patterns do you share?
7. From this moment onward, recognize when you are being a martyr. Why are you doing it?
8. Create a list of basic needs. Write all of the things that make you happy. Honor that list by not allowing others to steal opportunities to fulfill those needs.
9. How can you make your life more ideal? What is one thing you

can do TODAY?

RELEASE Martyr Scoundrel Mentality with the following Affirmations:

- ॐ *It is okay for me to be a priority to myself.*
- ॐ *People appreciate and respect me.*
- ॐ *I am valued simply for being me.*
- ॐ *I serve the world best after taking care of my needs.*
- ॐ *My life is balanced between taking care of my needs and taking care of others.*
- ॐ *The more I give myself the more I can give others.*
- ॐ *My opinion of myself matters to me.*
- ॐ *I love and approve of myself.*
- ॐ *It is easy to express myself.*
- ॐ *I can say no without losing love or approval.*
- ॐ *I am in harmony with the Universe.*

Put Yourself First

Putting yourself first may seem selfish, but it's actually one of the most selfless things we can do.

Until you have lavished upon yourself love, attention, kindness, sweetness, appreciation and rest, don't bother lavishing anyone else with what you don't have to offer them.

Before setting off on a flight, the flight attendant will inform us that in case of an emergency, we should place our own oxygen masks on before assisting others. Why should we do that? Isn't that a terribly selfish thing to do? After all, by not wasting time putting on our oxygen masks, we can assist other people immediately. And we should each be able to help at least a dozen people before we run out of oxygen. But what if we spent the first thirty seconds in a flight emergency putting on our own masks? We won't be able to reach other people immediately, but there's a great chance we'll be able to assist every person on the entire plane as well as save ourselves. We would be heroes and live to tell about it.

Now, apply this analogy to your life. How often do you sacrifice your happiness to help someone else? What have you given up for the well-being of your family and friends? Do you resent giving those things up? Do you feel like it was your choice or did you feel pressured or obligated to do it?

Let go of whatever resentment you are holding and move into the present moment. What can you do today that will prove that you are number one to you?

People who make a daily commitment to yoga or meditation are doing a great thing for themselves and for every single person with whom they come in contact. They are taking time to get centered, grounded and focused. They are releasing their tension and stress. They are inhaling deeply and fully, bringing positive, healing energy into their bodies and exhaling toxins. They are taking a few moments to find peace and they can spread that peace to everyone they meet.

That is the result of taking time to honor yourself and put yourself first.

Think of how you feel after spending an hour in traffic or in an enormous crowd. Your anxiety level and blood pressure may rise and your breathing may shallow. Your nervous system is stimulated, making you feel unsettled and more jittery.

Now think about how you feel when you do something you love and for which you have great passion. Thinking about this activity or actually doing it will reduce your stress level, calm your breathing and bring harmony to your body. Revel in that energy.

Your reactions to the events of your day are carried to all the people with whom you come in contact. This is why it's necessary for us to put ourselves first. When we are happy, we can impart that happiness to others. Rather than bring anger and anxiety into the world, bring more peace and happiness to it by finding peace and happiness for yourself first.

Direct Communication

Martyr Scoundrels tend to have a fear of what other people will think of them. They have a fear of disapproval. This is why conversations that need to be held are not held. Recognize how much easier it is to go directly to the source of the issue rather than discussing the issue with everyone else. If you have a leak in your kitchen pipe, you wouldn't simply ignore it, nor would you put a bucket under it and hope that it goes away. You wouldn't pay attention to every other pipe in your home and avoid the pipe that is leaking. You would fix the leak by attending to the leaking pipe. You would get help if you needed it. You would deal with the pipe in a positive, favorable, level-headed way, rather than get angry and take a hammer to it. Moving calmly and compassionately and speaking in this same manner will allow things to flow smoothly and beautifully.

Be open and honest. Always speak directly to the person you need to talk to, without involving other people. Do not avoid the one person with whom you're having the problem.

Speak with compassion. Put yourself in the other person's shoes. How would you want to be treated? Would you appreciate someone being completely honest with you? Or would you rather have someone hide their feelings to avoid potentially uncomfortable conversations and instead tell everyone except you how they are feeling?

Speak from the heart. Begin sentences with "I feel" and "I need." Avoid sentences such as "You make me" and "You always."

One of the issues with Martyr Scoundrels is being unable to say "No." They take on duties with obligation rather than joy. The energy that needs to be added into the world is an energy of joy, not dread, obligation, loathing and unhappiness. By continuing to do things out of obligation, we are adding to the negative energy in the Universe. By accepting the responsibilities and opportunities in which we truly want to participate, we add to the joy of the Universe. Expressing ourselves and our needs helps others to express themselves, too. A great deal of fear may arise, as well as feelings of vulnerability, but instead of hiding our emotions, we can release them through our words in direct communication. This will empower you and others. It will make us more courageous. It will bring us into balance. It will release us from obligation and dread.

For years, "Carol" refused to speak her mind. She didn't speak much as a child. She shied away from strangers, although she never had a problem volunteering to answer questions in the classroom. As an editor for her college newspaper, she had an opportunity to write a twice weekly column, but choose not do it. She found ways of expressing herself indirectly rather than share her true feelings. Carol avoided debate. Only when she felt secure with someone would she directly and honestly communicate.

How does Carol benefit from not communicating with others? She doesn't have to face rejection or ridicule because she does not share her innermost thoughts and feelings with anyone. People accept her and enjoy her easy-going nature. Failing to communicate has been a great form of protection for Carol.

But Carol is suffering from holding on to this old pattern because by not communicating, she fails to open her heart. She has spent many years alone, feeling isolated because she did not want to be hurt. When Carol was in a relationship with someone, her needs were left unmet because she never shared what they were. She developed chronic bronchitis as a result of cutting off her communication and closing her throat chakra.

When Carol is ready to let go of this negative pattern, she begins by visualizing what her life will be like after releasing her failure to communicate. She makes a physical representation of this by drawing a picture of herself connecting to people around her. Carol visualizes communicating with people one hundred percent from her heart and soul. She feels the ease of communicating with others. Every time she has an opportunity to speak her truth, she does her best communicating what she needs to say.

You can write or say positive affirmations to replace your old pattern. To become a better communicator, Carol affirms: "It is safe to speak my truth. People appreciate what I have to say. I am grateful for every opportunity to express myself." There might still be times when she doesn't fully communicate, but she later visualizes herself saying what she hadn't been able to say.

Over time, Carol discovers the ease of honest communication. She experiences the benefits of speaking her truth, which helps reinforce her desire to communicate. Now it seems strange to Carol that she ever had a communication issue. Relationships with others come easily for her now and she no longer needs to isolate herself from others.

It is also important to be aware of how you express yourself. If you have difficulty communicating, you may prefer to write a message or letter. Now that you have accepted the challenge of direct communication, it is important to vocalize what it is you need to say. It is very empowering to use your voice. If you feel more comfortable writing than speaking, write things first and then speak them later. This can be a very helpful way to make certain you say everything that you need to say. It keeps things brief and helps to avoid unnecessary words that express weakness or nervousness. Power is perceived in brevity. Weakness tends to come in length.

Singing, taking voice lessons, giving speeches or presentations, calling out bingo numbers, being a disc jockey, a community education teacher, an emcee, a tour guide or taking on any opportunity to use your voice can also be very empowering and help with direct communication. Step out of your comfortable box and begin to grow and expand with your voice and your truth.

Recall a particular time in the past when you had difficulty speaking your truth. What did you do? Did you talk to everyone about your issue? Did you suppress everything? Did you avoid saying the most difficult things? What could you have done differently?

Replay the situation in your mind or out loud in private. Allow the conversation to play through – even though you can only communicate your side. This action alone can be very liberating. Another option is to write a letter to the other person. Write everything without censor. Let your feelings pour onto the page. Write the letter from your heart, with the thought that the person you are writing the letter to will never read it. Read the letter when you're finished. Could you give it to the person? If not, write a second letter from a place of compassion. Write this letter as if the other person will some day read it. Again, read the letter when you're finished. Could you send this letter? If you could and you think this letter will be beneficial to the other person, send it. If not, keep it, burn it or tear it up. Simply writing the letter helps to recognize your thoughts and feelings and offers you some release.

Now that the letter has been written, you may also find that you are better equipped to have a conversation with the other person. Allow for that conversation to happen as quickly as you are able. Use that empowering energy to clear the situation. The sooner the conversation can occur, the better. Think about that leaky pipe. Obviously, it would be better to fix it within twenty-four hours rather than three weeks later. The same holds for direct communication. Whatever you hold inside is damaging to you, to the other person and to the Universal balance of energy. Repression stops your divine connection and divine flow of energy. The sooner you can clear the situation, the sooner you can return to harmony.

Compliment Yourself

Because many Martyr Scoundrels look outside themselves for approval, an important component to releasing this scoundrel is to gain self-approval. Complimenting yourself is a great way to do this.

What is it that you like about yourself? Write down a list of ten qualities that you admire in yourself. Put these qualities in statements that begin with, "I like _____." For example: "I like my creativity. I like my adventurous nature. I like my sense of humor. I like my positive attitude. I like my organization (compassion, generosity, carefree nature and musical skills)."

Avoid any qualities that describe a possession or association. Therefore, "I like my job as a teacher" could be changed to: "I like my ability to teach others." Change the phrase, "I like my children" into "I like my parenting skills."

Avoid using any qualities that are strictly physical such as, "I like my posture, my physique, my hands, my hair." Instead, focus on more intrinsic qualities.

Are you able to write ten compliments? Think about it for at least ten minutes if you cannot finish the list. If you are still stuck after ten minutes, put the list aside and give it more time. Do not ask anyone else what qualities they admire in you. Doing this enables your need to go outside of yourself for validation. This is an activity you need to do alone. Think about what qualities you admire in others. Can you find these qualities within yourself? Add them to your list. Remember that this list is for you. There are no right or wrong answers. After all, no one knows you like you know yourself.

You can also turn your list of compliments into a list of affirmations. "I like my ability to teach others" can be written: "I am a great teacher." "I like my parenting skills" can become the affirmation: "I am a great parent." The ultimate affirmation for you is: "I love and approve of myself."

Keep your list of compliments and/or affirmations in your wallet, appointment book, or some place you will see them often. When you are feeling inadequate in any way, take a look at your list and smile! You are perfect as you are in this moment.

Develop Your Self-Worth with Money

Since most societies currently use some form of currency for the exchange of goods and services, it's important for Martyr Scoundrels to take a look at their relationship to money because it is often related to self-esteem and approval.

Are you earning an appropriate amount of money for your time, effort, ability, education and creativity? Are you able to spend money on yourself without guilt? Do you give money generously? Do you trust that you will always have enough money for what you need? Are you able to save or invest your money for the future?

Many people have an issue with at least one area regarding money. People typically become very serious about money, rather than allow it to be fun. The games of *Life* and *Monopoly* involve money. Players can traverse the game boards collecting and losing money without apprehension. But what if you played the game with real money? Would you still have the same lighthearted approach with every shake of the dice or spin of the wheel?

Take a moment to examine all areas of your relationship to money.

If you are employed outside of the home, do you feel you are financially well-compensated for your talents and time? If you are well-compensated for your abilities, are you also honored with appropriate vacation time, an ideal office space and treated with the respect that you deserve? Are you working in a job that you love? What steps can you take today to be more gratified? Can you ask for a raise? Can you ask for a promotion? Would you consider a job transfer, changing companies or changing jobs? Would you consider self-employment?

If you are self-employed, what step(s) could you take to improve your current situation? How comfortable are you with selling your products or services? Do you underprice your goods or services? When people give you money, do you like them to put it in your hand or on the table?

What is your opinion of money? Finish the sentence: Money is _____. What is/was your parents' opinions of money? What is your spouse's opinion of money? What is your son's/daughter's opinion of money?

How is your attitude toward spending money on yourself? Are you able to spend money without worry? Do you buy only the necessary things you need? How often do you buy yourself treats? When is the last time you bought yourself a treat? What was it? Do you allocate a certain amount of your budget for fun and entertainment?

Do you buy gifts and surprises for other people? Is it easier for you to spend money on yourself or on others? Is it more important to find bargains when you shop for yourself or for others? Do you donate money for worthy causes? What percentage of the time do you give money when someone asks for it?

Is money always available when you need it? Do you trust in the Universe to always provide you with what you need?

How is your attitude about saving and investing? How much of your income do you save or put in an investment opportunity each month? Are you planning for your future?

By answering the above questions, you can discover what areas, if any, you are having difficulty with regarding money. Take a step toward solving this issue. If you are deserving of a raise, ask for one. If you're self-employed and your prices aren't reflective of your time, education, experience and effort, then it's time to raise your prices. If you have difficulty being generous, determine a sum that you can joyously give away to a cause in which you believe. If you have trouble saving your money, enlist the help of an investment-savvy friend or a financial planner and put a percentage of your paycheck toward an untouchable asset. The sooner you deal with your issues surrounding money, the sooner your prosperity can grow.

The fear of not having enough money is a common scarcity belief. Erase these statements from your vocabulary to improve your flow of money:

"I don't have enough money."
"I'm broke."
"Money is tight right now."
"I need to save for a 'rainy day.'"
"Everything costs money."
"There is no such thing as a free lunch."
"It's always a struggle to pay the bills."
"It takes money to make money."

Here are a few Universal laws that can be demonstrated quite easily with money:

1. Trust that you will always have more than enough.
2. Be generous toward yourself and others. Allow that generosity to come back to you multiplied.
3. Have faith that your investments and endeavors are prosperous.
4. Determine fair compensation for your services and knowledge. Expect to receive the full value of your worth. If you value yourself highly, others will also.

Find a Higher Connection

Whether you believe in God, spirit guides, the infinite wisdom of the Universe, a guardian angel, Spirit, the Mahavatar Babaji of India, Mother Nature or whomever or whatever gives you guidance every day, it is important to have a connection to a higher power. This provides you with the comfort and confidence that you are not alone. It is a reminder that someone, somewhere is always watching out for your best interest. And as we continue on the technological wave that we're on, where text messages and e-mails eliminate the need for face to face conversations, it's nice to know we have someone with us always. It lets us know we are loved unconditionally. It helps to guide us to the right place at the right time. It leads us to the ideal circumstances and toward the people we need to meet.

How does that help us release our Martyr Scoundrels? If we are looking for unconditional approval we can find it in ourselves and in our higher power. It can also help us in situations where we enter a room with no familiar faces. That can be a scary situation. Now, imagine that you enter the room with your best friend next to you who will always approve of you. Do you feel more at ease? More willing to open up and meet people?

Believing in a higher power gives us the ability to call upon it in any situation. It means you will never enter a room full of strangers alone. You will never face any situation you can't handle without some sort of guidance. The comfort from a higher power is astounding. And what a boost to our self-esteem to know that we are always loved and protected no matter what we have done. Wow!

Take time today to acknowledge a higher power. Think about a time when you are certain it played a role in your life. Express your gratitude. And next time you feel scared or alone or you are looking outside of yourself for approval, remember that your higher power is always available – whether you remember to call upon it or not.

Release Inhibition

Martyr Scoundrels, who honor others before themselves, typically carry a great deal of inhibition and worry about what others might think. It is not our problem what other people think of us. Therefore, we can release their thoughts and their judgments. This can allow us to think and move on our own accord, listening to our inner voices and our hearts.

"Kyle" refused to do yoga outside for fear of someone seeing him and thinking he was a New Age freak. He had a huge passion for yoga and for the outdoors and he wanted to combine his passions, but he allowed his inhibition to control him. And then one day, he was asked to do a photo shoot and there wasn't enough indoor lighting. They needed to take the photos outside, near a street that commanded fairly steady traffic. The necessity of the situation prevailed over his self-consciousness.

Within a few weeks, Kyle practiced yoga outside, regardless of who might see him. He realized that it was what he wanted to do and so he decided to do it. He also realized that the more he can be visible doing yoga, the more people will be exposed to it and consider doing yoga.

If we continue to move about in our daily lives worrying about what others will think of us rather than following our truest desires, we will have a society where everyone is ruled by peer pressure. To live in contentment, we need to follow our passions that are in line with our highest good.

Ask yourself what things you would add to your life if no one were around to judge you. Maybe you would only cut your grass once or twice a season. Maybe you would tear up your entire lawn and plant green beans and sunflowers. Maybe you would draw cartoon heroes all day. Maybe you would quit your current job and start your own business doing something you've fantasized about for years.

Maybe you would wear mismatched clothes or wear evening formal wear. Maybe you would grow your hair long, color it purple, shave it all off or never shave again. Maybe you would start up more conversations with strangers. Perhaps you'd go on more adventures, take more risks and move beyond uniformity.

Perhaps you'd follow your heart instead of following your society.

Imagine you are alone on earth. You can envision yourself out in the wilderness or in a metropolis. It is only you and other animals moving about the world. Everyone else is sleeping. You are free to do as you please without any social consequences whatsoever. No one will judge you, stare at you, question you or reprimand you.

So, what would you like to do that you otherwise wouldn't?

We stay locked in our comfort zones and societal norms because we learn to do what is acceptable by our peers. We have a fear of disapproval, of being different, of setting our own guidelines and honoring our truest passions. These fears have been programmed in us and they run deep.

It's time to break out of these societal controls.

Think of the craziest thing you would love to do and visualize yourself doing it. See the smile on your face that fulfills the depth of your soul. Then go do it.

Focus on your heart and spirit while being aware of not overstepping other people's boundaries. If my heart is screaming to dance and I blare my music at three a.m. and wake all my neighbors, I won't be serving my neighbors very well. It would be better if I play it semiloud and dance naked and free while my neighbors stayed asleep.

In most cases, breaking free from your comfort zone will have little adverse effect on anyone else. More likely, breaking out of your comfort zone will shake other people loose from theirs — whether anyone sees you uninhibited or not. Your energy will be different and the energy that you cast into the Universe will be different. This is all that is needed to move others from their rigid constructs.

Continually ask yourself what it is you want to be doing. And then move forward without regard of other people's opinions.

6
Negative Thinking Scoundrel

In most situations, Negative Thinking Scoundrels assume the worst. They are pessimistic and view life with skepticism. They feel unlucky and incompetent in at least one area of their life. They may be good at their job, but bad at sports. They might be talented artists, but they have no social skills.

Many of their negative thoughts are unconscious, such as *I am unlovable, I am wrong/bad* and *People disappoint/hurt me.* Obviously, these mantras are self-sabotaging and make their lives more difficult. The unconscious lies that play in their heads act as a constant deterrent in life. They may go to great lengths to avoid what is unfamiliar to them.

It can be emotionally and energetically draining to spend a great deal of time with Negative Thinking Scoundrels. Their negativity may not be obvious at first because many negative statements made by them are acceptable statements in society. It's not uncommon to hear someone say, "It's really difficult to do that" or "That kills me." T*hat* can refer to anything that expands their comfort zones, such as exercising, saving money, directly communicating, ending a bad habit or beginning a new habit. These negative statements are often said unconsciously because they are deeply rooted in our collective and individual consciousness. Because these negative statements are quite common, whoever is talking with Negative Thinking Scoundrels may agree with the negative statements without a second thought. This creates even more negative energy in the world.

Instead, these negative statements need to be uprooted like weeds. Every time one pops up, it needs to be recognized and turned into a positive statement.

Without anything to say and a lack of common ground with a stranger, these scoundrels will talk about bad weather, their bad health (this is especially common with aging Negative Thinking Scoundrels) or something negative in the world, like a war or a depressed economy. Most are completely unaware of this pattern. If they were able to recognize it, many would stop.

When you notice Negative Thinking Scoundrels in yourself or in others, switch the conversation to a positive subject or make only positive statements. For example, if Larry calls himself a moron, say "You're an intelligent man, Larry." Remind him of something he did successfully. Recognize even the slightest negative statements that you or someone else makes. "That'll be really hard," can become "That's a great opportunity." Never shame yourself for having had a negative thought or statement. Simply recognize and replace them.

Find the positive spin on everything that you say. Help others to be positive with compassion and grace, without becoming a "do good Pollyanna." If your positive statements don't alter the negativity of Negative Thinking Scoundrels, spend less time around them. If it's a family member or co-worker that you simply cannot avoid, continue to stay positive for the both of you.

Comfort and happiness come unconsciously to Negative Thinking Scoundrels by voicing their negativity, especially when someone else commiserates with them. They also find joy during brief moments of being positive and when they are surrounded by others with a positive outlook.

Comments you might hear from Negative Thinking Scoundrels:

"I can't..."
"I'm stupid."
"That was stupid."
"That won't work."

"Life is hard."
"Life is short."
"I'm getting old."
"I hate..."

If you OBSERVE and VERIFY the Negative Thinking Scoundrel in your life, EXAMINE the following:

1. How has the Negative Thinking Scoundrel helped you?
2. How has it negatively affected you?
3. To the best of your recollection, when were you first introduced to the Negative Thinking Scoundrel? Is this a family, cultural or societal scoundrel you consciously or unconsciously accepted as your own?
4. What are some examples of how you've been a Negative Thinking Scoundrel in the past week?
5. On a scale of one to ten, ten being the best, how would you rate your overall level of satisfaction and happiness in life?
6. In your circle, who else is visited by the Negative Thinking Scoundrels? Whom do you find yourself being negative with most often?
7. From this moment onward, recognize when you are negative. Switch your focus to being positive. How does your outlook change when you are more positive?
8. How can you make your life more ideal? What is one thing you can do TODAY?

RELEASE Negative Thinking Scoundrel Mentality with the following Affirmations:

🕉 *My positive thoughts produce positive results.*
🕉 *I trust that the Universe has a divine plan for me.*
🕉 *When I take a step in the right direction, opportunities appear.*
🕉 *Positive energy attracts positive people and situations.*
🕉 *I am a magnet for everything that is for my highest good.*
🕉 *All is well in my world.*

ॐ *I am intelligent.*
ॐ *I can accomplish anything.*
ॐ *I have all that I need right now.*

Avoid Negative Chatter

Often we apologize for ourselves, chatter negatively to ourselves or about ourselves to others, or preface our creations and ideas by slighting our abilities. In small and seemingly insignificant ways, we downplay our good qualities without even realizing it. For instance, imagine you baked your friend a pie. Your friend tells you it looks fabulous. You say, "Aw, it's nothing." In one quick second, you have downplayed an hour of your time, your talent, your accomplishment, and your friend's judgment. You've insulted yourself and your friend with your curt reply and you've wasted every thought, action and breath that went into making that pie.

Now take this example further. Imagine that you spent six months on a long-term project for work or six months making a quilt. When you are complimented for your effort, are you going to reply that it's nothing? Are you going to insult yourself on this large scale? Perhaps you might. Accepting compliments gracefully, with a smile and a "thank you," can be challenging for all scoundrels, especially Negative Thinking Scoundrels. You recognize the hard work that you've done and you want others to recognize it as well, but you want to be humble. That's what society taught us to do. Even though it would be polite to smile and give a word of thanks, we have become programmed to diminish what we've done. Again, we say, "It was nothing."

It doesn't really seem like a big deal, does it? But the Universe is very literal. So is your mind. What they both hear is: *Six months of my life that I poured into this project is nothing.* And they begin to recalibrate projects you have done in comparison to that. Soon, a great deal of your life turns into "nothing." And the bigger message your mind conveys to you is, *What you do means nothing,* which can also become *I do nothing.* Imagine what you will draw to yourself with that unconscious thought.

Negative Thinking Scoundrels, who are characteristically pessimistic, will scoff at this idea. They might think it's too far-fetched. And then they will later wonder why they haven't had a raise in six years and why strangers have stopped asking them what they do for a living. They are attracting these situations with their thought, *I do nothing.*

Look at other ways you talk negatively about yourself. "I did the stupidest thing yesterday…I would have remembered to get peanut butter at the grocery store if I weren't so scatter-brained…I'm such a slow reader, it'll take me two months to read that book…I'll never be able to make this putt…" Examine your self-talk. Become conscious of how you refer to yourself when you are alone and when you are in the presence of others. Squash the negative, nitpicking, critical judge inside of yourself. You would never talk to your friends this way, would you? If you did, and they had healthy self-esteem, you wouldn't have many friends left.

Take a moment and think of a few examples of how you've insulted yourself in the last twenty-four hours. Now visualize yourself saying these things positively. Your challenge each day is to speak and think positively about yourself. See if you catch yourself in any negative chatter.

Next time you insult yourself, no matter how seemingly small or inconsequential it seems, find a way to turn the insult around. Instead of saying, "I'm such a slow reader, it'll take me two months to read that book…" say "I'm sure I'll absorb the details of this novel since I savor every word." Instead of saying: "I would have remembered to get the peanut butter at the grocery store if I weren't so scatter-brained" say: "Next time I'll make a list so I'll remember the peanut butter."

Remember, if you wouldn't say the remark to your best friend, boss, client, priest, mother, etc., don't say it to yourself.

Obviously, it will not work to have lasting happiness if we are holding onto a lot of negative thoughts. Recognize your negative thoughts and replace those thoughts with positive ones. If your thoughts are not harmoniously aligned, your life will not operate from a place of continual contentment. We wouldn't cultivate a garden with junk and we shouldn't fuel our minds with garbage, either.

By getting internally clear by purifying your mind from negative, defeating thoughts, you can bring your words, actions and energy to a level of joy where no scoundrel can seize hold.

Recognize Your Accomplishments

What spectacular feats have you done in your life? What awards have you achieved? What contests have you won? Did you graduate from high school? College? Graduate school? Do you have a rewarding career? Have you read a lot of books? Are you knowledgeable on a particular subject? What physical achievements have you attained? Have you ever climbed a mountain? Have you won a tournament? A race? Are you in good health? Can you walk a mile? Run a mile? Can you ride a bike? Do you sing well? Where have you traveled to? Have you been a volunteer? Have you helped others? Do you have a successful marriage? Do you have healthy children? Do you have good friendships? Do people enjoy being around you? What hobbies do you have? Do you share them with others? Are you a good storyteller? Do you have a green thumb? Have you ever grown a plant? Planted a tree? Can you knit? Sew? Build a dog house?

What do you do well?

Take time to figure out what you have achieved in your life. Write down everything, no matter how small or insignificant it may seem and no matter how long ago it was. Include that wall mural you helped paint years ago or that unique Halloween costume you made last year. Add to your list as you remember things or accomplish new things.

This list is a visual representation of all the good things you have done so far in your life. No doubt, there are many things that you have written down, and many more things that you haven't considered or that you may have forgotten.

Often we focus on things we'd like to accomplish or things that we have failed at. These things tend to stick in our minds more than our past success. But right now, focus on what you have already done successfully. Writing this list may feel like bragging. We learn in our society that this is a negative thing and that we should be careful not to "toot our own horn" or we'll "get a big head." However, it's important to recognize our triumphs in life. In fact, when we don't stop to say to ourselves, *Wow, that was really incredible that I did that,* we often find ourselves getting wrapped up in more and more activities than we need to be in, senselessly running in circles and never feeling as though we've truly accomplished anything.

We begin to feel unworthy or not quite where we need to be yet. We think we'd be a better person, if only... *If only I could make a little more money. If only I could run faster. If only I could lose that last five pounds.* (This is similar to an aspect of Delayed Gratification Scoundrels, who project their happiness to the moment *when* they make more money, *when* they run faster, *when* they lose that last five pounds.) We fail to appreciate that we're currently earning the most we've ever earned, or that we can run at all, or that we are at a pretty healthy weight right now. When we fail to see our true inner qualities, we keep doing things in an attempt to gain self-worth.

This doesn't mean you have to spend the rest of your life without goals. It doesn't mean you never have to *do* anything again because you've already accomplished such a long list of achievements. If you choose to meditate or renounce the physical world, that is up to you. It isn't wrong to want to make more money or run faster or lose weight. But before you focus on what you're not, focus on what you are.

Otherwise when are you going to stop and appreciate what you have or what you've done so far? When are you going to feel like you're good enough? When are you going to approve of yourself, increase your self-esteem and happiness?

After you have written your list, read through it again. Read through it every time you doubt yourself – when you think you are not smart enough, not as good as someone else or when you avoid speaking your mind because you think your opinion is unimportant. Whenever you look at this list, know that yes, you have wonderful things to contribute to the world around you. You are valuable and talented!

Alter Your Perception

Every moment of every day, we can choose to live in joy, gloom or anywhere between these two emotional states. We can choose to be content, happy, indifferent, anxious, stressed, fearful, angry, sad, depressed, harried, lethargic, downtrodden, lucky, unlucky, picked on, beaten down or overworked. We can choose our reality and our emotional state.

Make a conscious choice to be happy. Sometimes the difference between joy and misery for any activity or for life, in general, is simply a matter of choice. You can be miserable while cleaning the bathtub or you can be happy. The situation does not change, only your perception does.

Stress can lead to heart attacks, heart disease, obesity, cancer, autoimmune diseases and many other issues. Stress manifests in our physical bodies over time. It is not what happens to us that causes us stress, but how we *react* to it. We can be miserable or we can be joyful.

In most situations with which we are faced, we can move to a place of gratitude and replace our misery. For example, if you're upset that your grocery store only has green bananas that won't be edible for three or four days, you can replace your disappointment with the gratitude that you are able to buy the bananas even if they're not edible right now. You can be grateful that you'll be able to indulge in your bananas in a few days. You can be glad that you are able to get everything else on your list. You can be glad that you'll have food on the table, food in your kitchen cupboards, in your pantry and in your refrigerator. Realize that not everyone on earth has the luxury of obtaining everything on their grocery list. Not everyone on earth has been inside a grocery store or eaten a banana.

In 2000, I stayed with a family in Bulgaria for a few days. I asked the mother what the differences were in Bulgaria now that it is no longer Communist. She told me there wasn't much difference. They were a poor family during Communism and they are poor now. There was no work then and there is no work now. She said it didn't matter much whether her country was Communist or not. But as she paused for a moment, she realized one difference: now there were no bananas.

It seems like a small thing. For someone who doesn't like bananas it is inconsequential whether they exist at all or whether they are green or yellow. But for someone who needs bananas to make banana bread for a charity bake sale or to make their child's favorite birthday cake, not having them available can be disappointing.

But it isn't as terrible as not having the option to eat anything at all.

For many of us, green bananas are a nice lesson in patience and creativity. We could wait a few days for our bananas to be more edible. We could put the bananas in a paper bag in the sun and make them ripen faster. Or we could shop at another store for yellow bananas.

This example with bananas is simple. But you can take the same principles of perception and apply them to situations of bigger consequence. Perhaps instead of reacting to green bananas it is reacting to the loss of a job or a flooded house. If you overreact because the bananas are too green at the store, how will you react in a bigger situation or a real emergency?

How we react to the little things that we experience in daily life – unexpected weather, traffic, misplacing our keys – help us to deal with bigger situations. No matter how we choose to perceive the situation, it still exists. What do we have to gain by being annoyed? We will be successful in adding negative energy to ourselves, the people around us and the Universe. Our negative energy and increased stress level caused our heart beat and our blood pressure to increase and our cortisol levels to rise, all of which can add to physical illnesses.

It is much more beneficial to maneuver through situations without reaction. Take action instead. Either buy the green bananas or don't. Go to another store or don't. See the bright side of the situation without letting it affect you.

Make a conscious choice to act. Don't react. Reaction comes from a place of fear. Visualize zebras, hyenas, lions and leopards in the wild. What usually happens when they react?

They die.

What happens when they act?

They prosper.

Essentially, our negative, toxic thoughts and reactions will kill us as well. The longer we choose to deal with situations where we react, the less we prosper. The longer we choose to foster negative thoughts, the less we prosper.

Most everyone has had difficult, stressful times where little things have affected them and fear has arisen. Getting stressed over a few minor details in life won't help you, but it isn't likely to put you in your grave. But react with extreme emotions for sixty or seventy years and they will.

What would you do in the following situations?

- Another driver takes your turn at a four-way stop.
- You break your favorite lamp.
- You get a parking ticket on a street where a "permit only" sign was blocked by trees.
- You discover someone has stolen money from you.
- Your best friend lied to you.

Would you swear? Get angry? Yell? Cry? Complain to friends or family knowing they will console you? Do you lose your faith in humanity, authority or yourself?

In your mind's eye, observe your response to each situation without judgment. Maybe you've been in some of these situations or you've been in something similar to them. After you reflect on each situation and your hypothetical response, think about your ideal responses. Are they the same? What would you need to do differently in order to respond the way you would like to?

In the first example, maybe you can visualize yourself getting angry and swearing at the other driver. But if you're having a bad day, you might say, "You stupid driver, you need to learn to wait your turn!" You might add a few derogatory names in your tirade and honk your horn.

How do we stay content in this situation?

We don't react. We trust in the Universe and in karma. We don't need to ingest stress from the situation. Put yourself in the other person's shoes. Maybe the driver didn't realize it wasn't his turn. Maybe he is late for an appointment. It's not your problem that he's late, but if we extend compassion to him, we will accept his premature turn. He only delayed you three or four seconds. Will it really make any difference to your day or to your life? Not at all.

Breaking your favorite lamp might have a slightly bigger effect on your day or your life, but it is a material item. No matter how much you love the lamp, it's not worth your stress and the adverse effects to your health. Your longevity and vitality will be better without reaction and attachment to material possessions. The parking ticket can be paid or debated in court. There's bound to be some internal lesson about noticing details from the situation no matter what you choose to do about it.

Being stolen from or lied to are acts that need careful consideration. Look at your core negative beliefs regarding these acts. Do you have a belief that you don't get your fair share? That people hold out (money or truth) on you? It's important to set some boundaries. Have a conversation with your friend and, if possible, with the person who stole the money.

In every situation, you can also be grateful. Be glad that you are safe and alive, that your car is safe, that you didn't break your arm, burn down your house or lose your entire life savings.

You can spend your life thinking that you never get a fair deal. You can believe that people are only out for themselves. Or you can appreciate your life. You can recognize all the good and bad as equal and learn lessons from every experience. You can change your perception and move to a place of happiness and gratitude. You can realize that you have everything that you need in this moment and there is no need to wait to have your needs met. You are fulfilled at all times in all ways.

Choose to act, but also choose to stay content. Strive for it.

Move with gratitude and graciousness. See the ways in which you prosper and flourish because of your contentment. Living in joy will uplift your spirit and radiate into others. Your physical body will suffer no ill effects, your stress level will decrease and you will have a positive impact on the people around you.

Being joyful and calm doesn't mean you condone situations that are not ideal for you. Take action in whatever way you deem necessary. But do it in a way that doesn't negatively affect you. Do it in a way that leaves you feeling joyful that you spoke your mind. Confront with compassion and love.

See yourself in every person who crosses your path. Also, observe yourself. Notice when you are stressed and tired from waiting in line. Notice when you scowl or frown. Notice when your heart races and your blood pressure goes crazy with inner turmoil. Are you okay with how that feels inside your body, how it looks to others and how it effects your day and your life?

Learn how to perceive "negative" situations differently so that they are no longer negative. Allow "bad" situations to become good. Find the enjoyment in every situation. Or change the situation or your perception. Don't remain in what doesn't feel right or good. Continually strive for contentment.

Release Your Scarcity Mentality

As human beings able to create our reality and manifest our dreams, we only lack where we are blocking ourselves or where something is not in our highest good. The concept of scarcity, of not having enough or lacking something, is able to exist only when we disconnect ourselves from the abundance of the Universe. If we choose to focus on what we are lacking (like anything else we focus our energy on), we will create more lack for ourselves in that area. *Belief in lack equates to fear.* Having a scarcity mentality is like having an altar of fear. You might as well worship and physically bow to your fear because you are mentally bowing to it every day.

Instead, focus on abundance. Focus on limitless desires. Focus on creating whatever it is you most want that is for your highest good. Believe that it is already yours.

Negative thinking scoundrels who have a scarcity mentality often come to resent anyone who possesses what it is they desire. Envy takes them away from living a happy life. Envy makes them resentful. It takes them to a place where negative energy dominates and leaves them even further from possessing whatever it is they believe they are lacking. Envy is another form of fear. If they react with jealousy, they are afraid that they are not good enough unless they have the thing they desire.

The fear of not having enough money is a common scarcity belief (Chapter Five: Martyr Scoundrels: Develop Your Self-Worth with Money.) Release the beliefs of your family, your friends and your society as a whole. Replace those negative, fear-based thoughts with thoughts of love and total fulfillment. Here are some common fear-based thoughts to avoid:

"I can't afford that."
"There are not enough good, available men or women around."

"We're running out of clean drinking water, (trees, oil, land, etc.)."
"There's never enough time."
"I don't have enough energy to do that."
"It's really difficult to get started."
"It's flu (cold) season. I'm bound to get what's going around."
"It's hell to get old."
"I'm too old to do that."
"I can't move like I used to."
"I'm dying to know..."
"It's killing me."

Let's examine some fear-based traps into which we can fall, including love, money, resources, time and energy.

Love

Love is absolutely limitless. You can love everybody and everything. You can love all the plants, all the animals and every physical object around you. You can love the clouds, the sun, energy, wind, water, fire, air and the earth. You can love your life, your reality, concepts, theories, inventions, scientific laws, society, authority and anarchy. Love is the emotion of power, confidence, ability and execution. Love is total connection and manifestation.

The more you can expand your circle, the more people you can love directly. You can love unconditionally. You can love without limitations. Your ability to love will exponentially rise when you expand your love of yourself. The more you can honor yourself, nurture yourself and fulfill your needs, the more your capacity to love the world around you and everyone in it will grow.

Love is immeasurable and limitless.

Money

Another false belief is that there is a scarcity of money. In America, the most recognized form of physical currency is created by the Federal Reserve and it is printed in a definite amount annually. But money can be created in any form we choose without counterfeiting. We need only be creative in order to create more money. Alternative monetary systems are in place throughout the world in which communities trade notes as currency for services and goods. Bartering is an exchange of goods and services. Communal living eliminates the need for money because each person in the community brings special talents to the group and food is grown on the land. There is also the possibility of manifestation without money. For example, you need a lawn mower, and your neighbors offer you an extra one that they no longer need. We can be creative in how we choose to manifest what we need in our lives without money.

Money, in this sense, is immeasurable and limitless.

Resources

To have unlimited resources, we need only create different energy sources than we currently have and use the alternative sources we have in existence now in a manner that is more economical and affordable to the masses. That does not mean wasting our current resources. It instead means promoting alternative, renewable and efficient fuel sources. Instead of worrying about current uses of energy, and how we waste it, we can concentrate efforts on environmentally sustainable sources. We can also invent more ways to produce energy from our waste.

Acknowledge the current situation for what it is. Bless it and trust that good will come from it. These actions help you to be a part of the solution rather than add to the negative energy of a scarcity mentality.

Our collective consciousness will determine how we manage our energy and other resources (food, paper, etc.). If we focus on the idea that we are running out of resources, we will run out of resources. If we focus on alternative resources and renewable resources, we will have many wonderful, economical, sustainable energy sources. If we trust in the Universe and Mother Nature and believe that the perfect solution will arise, it will arise.

Resources, especially the ones we don't yet know about, are immeasurable and limitless.

Time

People believe they never have enough time to do all that they would like to accomplish. They become frustrated when they are wasting time, such as waiting in a long line. Financial importance is placed on time with the thought: *Time is money.*

We measure time through the base unit of a second. We measure it with watches and clocks, the position of the sun, the tides, the seasons and the years. If we were to throw away all time devices outside of the natural world, we would lose the precision of the second, the minute and the hour. Time would become relative, passing slowly or quickly depending on our activity. During meditation and sleep, we may lose all concept of time.

Because we are not born knowing the exact time we will depart the world, time can be seen as limited or limitless. It is our choice of how we want to view this. We can, however, discover the limitlessness of time by picking a particular activity, like golfing. If we choose to do nothing else but golf for as long as we desire, we will have limitless time to golf.

Without technological precision, time is immeasurable and limitless.

Energy

Energy is the ability to do work. We may find ourselves seeking energy when our blood sugar is low, when we are sleep deprived or when we are bored. Operating from a scarcity mentality, we may seek energy when we think we should be low on energy, based on past experience rather than present circumstance. If we have a scarcity mentality, we will find ourselves seeking stimulants to boost our energy level, such as food, caffeine, adrenaline and fresh air. If we remain in a scarcity mentality, we put our faith in the physical realm.

If we alter our reality to one based in love, we can go directly to the Universe to manifest more energy. We can allow this energy to flow to us during meditation or by connecting with the elements. Or we can simply trust that we will receive an abundance of energy if it is for our highest good.

In a love-based reality, energy is immeasurable and limitless.

Examining each of these further, we can recognize that the list is comprised of infinite and immeasurable things. It is merely our thoughts that need to change in order to view these things as unlimited instead of limited.

Think about areas in your life in which you are currently lacking. What thoughts have kept you in this scarcity mentality? Break free from this trap by changing those thoughts to the most positive, limitless thoughts you can imagine. Allow your reality to change with the power of your mind. Be diligent with this exercise. Notice positive results that reinforce your positive thinking. If something negative happens, unearth the thought that allowed that situation to occur. Learn the lesson behind it as well. Keep your focus on the positive, allowing the best to come into your life.

7
Stuck in the Past Scoundrel

Resentment, anger, guilt and shame are strong emotions that fuel Stuck in the Past Scoundrels. Those who have not released past wrongs done to them or past wrongs which they have done are energetically and emotionally bound to the people, places and events involved in these past dramas. Releasing the people or events that have hurt us liberates us and frees the energy that was attached to the resentment.

Releasing past unhappy events is healing. The past has already occurred. It is technically unchangeable. Reliving our unhappy pasts in our minds, our bodies and our spirits keeps us unhappy. Harboring grudges and storing resentment is like inviting tapeworms to take up residence in our intestines.

Releasing choices we have made, whether the results were good or bad, is also very liberating. Debating whether you made the right choice twenty years ago when you took a job in another state is quite harmful to you as well. The choice you made twenty years ago is now an irrevocable choice. Expect that the choice you made was indeed the right one and move forward. Or accept that it might not have been the best choice for you, but your path has since realigned based on the new parameters.

Every move you make can shift your reality. As you make decisions in the present, check in with your heart and your higher power. Make the choice that feels right. Trust that you are always led in the right direction. Trust that if there happens to be a few wrong choices along your path, it will get recalibrated. Don't sit and dwell on what is past and now unchangeable. Spending one ounce of energy on the thought: *What would have happened if* ... is redundant. Recycling this repetitive, dead end thinking is about as productive as harboring negative energy.

We are energetic beings. By releasing our unhappy past and our energetic connection to the past, we are able to experience more happiness and joy. By keeping our energy tied to unhappy emotions and an unhappy past, we keep ourselves unhappy.

Often these scoundrels are stuck reliving trauma from their childhood. Perhaps they were abused or molested or they were treated unfairly by family members, peers or other adults. To continue allowing the past wrongs done to them to ruin their current and future lives is as great a tragedy as the original incident.

Stuck in the Past Scoundrels find happiness in the space between reliving unhappy memories of the past. They may also find comfort in their stubborn willpower to refuse to forgive or release the past, but this is actually a mistaken comfort, like an unhealthy addiction.

If our resentment, anger, guilt or shame can be remedied through action, then take action. Write a letter, write in a journal or have a conversation to release emotions that tie you to unhappy past events. The journal or letter can be written with the intent that you are the only reader of either. They can be burned after they are written. The conversation can be with anyone who acts as a surrogate if you are unable to speak with the actual person involved. The important thing is that you are able to release the past in whatever method works best for you.

Comments you might hear from Stuck in the Past Scoundrels:

"I will never forgive..."
"Someday, I'll show them."
"If only I'd done (this) instead of (that), my life would be much better."
"I can't get that horrible image out of my head."
"I'm not sure you can ever undo what you've done."
"My life has gone downhill ever since..."

If you OBSERVE and VERIFY the Stuck in the Past Scoundrel in your life, EXAMINE the following:

1. How has the Stuck in the Past Scoundrel helped you?
2. How has it negatively affected you?
3. To the best of your recollection, when were you first introduced to the Stuck in the Past Scoundrel? Is this a family, cultural or societal scoundrel you consciously or unconsciously accepted as your own?
4. What are some examples of how you've been a Stuck in the Past Scoundrel in the past week?
5. On a scale of one to ten, ten being the best, how would you rate your overall level of satisfaction and happiness in life?
6. In your circle, who else is visited by the Stuck in the Past Scoundrels? Whom do you find yourself reminiscing with (or about) most often?
7. From this moment onward, recognize when you are stuck in the past. Why are you doing it? Are you bored? Are you angry?
8. How can you make your life more ideal? What is one thing you can do TODAY?

RELEASE Stuck in the Past Scoundrel Mentality with the following Affirmations:

- ॐ *I choose to resolve past issues.*
- ॐ *I now recognize and release what is no longer in my highest good.*
- ॐ *I am ready to release old limitations.*
- ॐ *I forgive myself.*
- ॐ *I release any ill intent I have toward others.*
- ॐ *I forgive myself for anything I have done in my past.*
- ॐ *I release shame and guilt for any past situations of which I am not proud.*
- ॐ *I choose to let go of any person, thought or situation which is no longer serving me.*
- ॐ *I release the pain of my past.*

ॐ By releasing my resentment, I now allow abundance to come to me.

ॐ I am free and filled with peace in the present moment.

Don't Take Things Personally

Nearly every one carries their load of emotional baggage. Some of this baggage is the result of a past trauma from which they did not recover or which they did not forgive and release. This emotional baggage lingers around them, permeating their negative energy. They may have had a difficult childhood, a harried morning or are having a frustrating work day. They may be dealing with a sick child, a dying parent, a cheating spouse or financial problems. Sometimes this emotional baggage airs itself in imperceptible ways. Maybe it is released by honking at the driver going two miles under the speed limit or by avoiding holding open the door for someone, by not smiling or saying hello or by arguing for no apparent reason at all.

It is important that we don't take these actions personally. Unless someone makes a valid point through constructive criticism on how you could have improved something you did, it would serve you best to ignore the other person's action. Be certain you do not internalize someone else's emotional baggage. Carrying emotional baggage, however, does not give anyone the right to act rude. Do not allow other people to treat you poorly. Do not condone the other person's action.

In situations with strangers where you do not or cannot take the opportunity to discuss the situation, like while driving, shrug it off. When an acquaintance ignores you when you say hello, perhaps he didn't hear you, he is focused on something or he is weighted down with health problems. Presume it has nothing to do with you. Keep your self-esteem intact. Release the situation and move forward.

This principle of not taking things personally can help Stuck in the Past Scoundrels release issues that they've been holding onto for years. Abuse that they suffered as children was likely done by someone who had also been abused as a child. Peers that teased them in school were probably treated horribly by their siblings or parents.

Part of the reason why we are so upset that we were treated badly is because our egos don't like to be treated badly. Our egos want us to be princes and princesses every minute of the day, which is ironic because it is our egos that are the cause of separating us from living a charmed existence.

Remove yourself from the entire equation for a moment. "Scott Scooper's" biggest resentment in life was the relentless teasing he endured from his peers in grade school. The mere reminder of grade school makes him surly. The kids called him "Super Duper Pooper Scooper" and the boys in the rest room asked him if he was looking for a "Scooper Snack" in the stalls. There was also a long bout of teasing with whoopee cushions and rumors that he had pet dung beetles. Scott was a shy child who took everything personally and never forgot the teasing. He never understood why the other kids didn't get teased like he did, although in reality, Scott probably had peers who got teased worse.

Since we're not Scott, it's easy for us to look at this situation with a blasé or amused eye. Scott appears to be lucky that his only resentment in life comes from mild teasing in grade school and he was not physically or sexually abused. Likely, some of his teasers were. From the perspective of karma, Scott got off pretty easily regarding childhood trauma. That still does not make what his peers did right, but it should make it easier for Scott to stop taking his childhood teasing personally. The next section will help in releasing anger and resentment of the past.

Eliminate Resentment

What is it that you're angry about? When asked, many people would politely suggest they're not angry about anything. But if they were to dig deep enough, they could uncover memories that make them irritated.

It's time to move that anger out of your body. Unresolved anger and resentment often get stored in the lower back. It manifests as a feeling of not being supported, as someone or something that has done you wrong. Just as stress can cause an ulcer, unresolved anger can cause lower back issues. Storing resentment, or anything else that is negative in the body, eliminates room for healthy positive energy.

What if you're not sure if you have stored resentment? If you really can't think of anything that you resent, it might be pushed deep down because resentment is not something we want to surface in our daily lives. But it's easy to see how much anger and resentment you are carrying. Observe your attitude or your emotional state when you're in a hurry at the grocery store and you've picked the slowest line by several minutes. Observe your attitude when you're driving behind someone who is going below the speed limit or when you discover a leak in your pipes or a flat tire on your car. Do you curse at the situation and wonder why such bad things happen to you? Do you curse at the other driver or the person in the grocery line writing a check or using too many coupons?

If that sounds like you, you've got stored resentment. Make a list of all the things you resent in your life. They can be silly and totally inconsequential things or they can be enormous, life-altering issues. Here's an example:

I resent having ruined a perfectly good lunch today because I left it on the burner too long. I resent the dogs getting their feet muddy outside today and tracking their footprints across the floor. I resent not finding a gas station at either of the highway exits I took. I resent having had three hours of sleep last night. I resent my friend not calling me. I resent when people mispronounce my name. I resent my high school French teacher mocking my accent in front of the whole class. I resent my Grandmother favoring other cousins over me...

The more time you spend on your list, the more resentment may arise. So, now what do you do with that? You certainly don't want to tarnish a perfectly good day by dragging yourself down with the realization that you've been pretty mad about a lot of things for a long time. Instead, it's time to release the resentment. Here's a three step plan on releasing resentment:

Step One: Acknowledge the resentment. Accept the feelings you had and know that you had a right to have them.

Step Two: Forgive yourself or anyone involved with that situation. This does *not* mean you condone the action. It means you release all energetic ties to the person and the past action.

Step Three: Release the resentment. If it is an ongoing resentment – one that you expect will return – figure out how to see to it that it doesn't. Will that require a change in perception or an explanation of your feelings through a conversation or letter (whether anyone is actually available to read it)? Do what you need to do so that you won't continue to harbor the same resentment for the same issue. Write a positive affirmation to release the resentment.

To further detail this three step plan, let's use the example, *I resent when people mispronounce my name.*

Step One: I resent when people mispronounce my name. This has happened since I was a young child. Taisa is not a common name and I have had numerous unwanted alibis: Taise, Tayahsa, Tessie, Taiso... Although I enjoy the uniqueness of my name, it bothers me that I have to correct people all the time and many people need to be corrected several times because they consistently say it wrong. I feel as though people don't care enough about me to take the time to learn how to say my name correctly.

Step Two: I forgive everyone who has ever mispronounced my name. I forgive myself for having been angry toward everyone who has ever mispronounced my name.

Step Three: I release the resentment I have harbored for people who have mispronounced my name. In the future, I will annunciate my name clearly and loudly. I will correct anyone who mispronounces my name the first time and not wait until the second or third mispronunciation. Affirmation: "My name is easy to pronounce. People remember my name correctly."

(Notice that the positive affirmation is not: *People no longer mispronounce my name.* The Universe, or the subconscious mind, will grab hold of the word mispronounce above all others because it is the focal point of the sentence. The result would be people still mispronouncing her name.)

Eliminating old resentment helps to release stored tension from your body and extinguish the power others have had over you. Continuing to be offended by grade school classmates for making fun of your name or your height does not serve your best interest. In no way are you "getting back" at them by harboring bad feelings toward them. Most likely they will have no idea if you have forgiven them. They may not even remember you.

Release the people involved to their highest good. Better to resolve the issue and move forward. Otherwise, you continue to expel energy by having an emotion toward them. Your energy gets tied to them and to the situation, keeping you from moving forward. Blaming others or harboring resentment sends a subconscious message to your body and soul that others control your emotions and your perception of events.

Choose three issues from your list and follow the three step plan with each issue. Choose three of the biggest issues from your list, which will help to remove a great deal of resentment.

Choose more than three issues if you like or return to this list at a later date and continue to work through the three step plan with other resentments. But be sure to pick three now and begin to release some of that pent up resentment. Resentment and happiness are inversely proportional. When one is high, the other is low. It's time to tip the Stuck in the Past Scoundrel off balance and move yourself in a favorable direction. Trust that you are now on a better path for yourself – focused in the present and unbound by anger, resentment or regret.

Release Blame

Rape, incest, murder, robbery, reckless driving, child abuse, domestic violence and other heinous crimes are unacceptable actions. Any actions of malevolence that harm another living creature are wrong. Those who have suffered through these crimes are not to be blamed. They should feel no guilt or shame for having suffered these acts.

Blaming others, however, solves nothing. Along with releasing resentment, it is important to release blame from your life.

After you have healed from a trauma, but are still holding blame, ask yourself: *What belief do I have that would cause something bad to happen to me? What negative thought am I holding?* People's issues and agendas sometimes intermingle and result in certain outcomes. Other people can do things to you that are inappropriate and wrong. But recognize that you are part of this equation. The problems that occur to you always have one common denominator: you.

Look inside yourself at what thought or belief needs to be cleared. Believing that you are bad, you are unlovable, you are guilty, you are too much, you are not enough, you are not good enough and you are separate from the Universe (God, Spirit) are thoughts and beliefs that can keep you stuck. Release them. Affirm: "I am divine. I am lovable. People love me. I love myself. I am innocent. I am enough." Ideally, look into a mirror, directly into the reflection of your eyes and repeat these statements. Continue to work with them until they are easy for you to say and you feel they are believable. If they seem like lies, keep saying them anyway. They are tiny seeds of brilliance you are planting into your psyche. And they are true for every individual's highest self. "Yes, your highest self is divine. Yes, your highest self is lovable…"

What thought do you need to clear if a co-worker is screaming at you for something beyond your control? Do you believe that peop treat you badly? Do you believe you are unlovable or not good enough? Do you believe you are bad and need to be punished? Do you believe that your life is cursed? Clear the most dominant of those negative thoughts and clear your pathway to bliss.

There may be some people who will push all of your buttons or who don't respect your boundaries. And there are times that we can look inside ourselves and see what they are reflecting in us and what lesson we can learn from their presence in our lives. There are times when we can use the opportunity to address these issues and discuss them directly with the person.

But there are other times where we aren't ready to recognize the lesson even if it appears to us in every direction we face, through every person we meet. Distance yourself from people and situations when you aren't willing or able to appropriately deal with them. You don't have to let everyone into your life. Use your intuition on what situations and people feel right for you.

It is also important to eliminate blaming people for making you feel a certain way. This idea gives your power to them, just as any negative emotion does. You are a unique individual. Your emotions are unique to you. No one can impose your feelings on you.

Many people find utter happiness and utter disappointment in their closest relationships. They expect their families, spouses and best friends to make them happy. (Read Chapter Three: Addicted to Misery Scoundrel: You Are Responsible for Your Happiness.) They blame their entire realm of emotions on other people. They become quick to blame others, God, the Devil, the weather, the government and the Universe when their realities do not reflect their aspirations. They take things personally and react to situations.

Do not blame anyone or anything for your happiness. Likewise, you wouldn't depend on someone to bring you into a place of anger, fear or sadness. We shouldn't expect other people to cater to any of our emotions. Nobody can make us feel any particular way. People's actions could *result* in us feeling happy, angry, afraid or sad. But we are responsible for our emotions. Watch statements such as: "You make me so angry." "You make me happy." "You make me sad." "Don't make me feel guilty."

Change these statements to: "I feel angry/happy/sad/guilty." And then release your anger, sadness and guilt. Ask yourself what boundaries have been crossed to make you feel angry. Discuss this directly with the person who crossed your boundaries. Clear it. Release guilt in all matters. You are divine and innocent. Apologize for your action(s). Retrace your steps in every possible way and bring yourself into the present moment. You are innocent right now. Feel that energy. Breathe it.

What will it take to release your sadness? Take action to move out of that feeling at the pace that feels right for you. Do what brings you joy. If you choose to remain stuck in your sadness, recognize that this is your choice. You own your perception and your pace.

For Stuck in the Past Scoundrels to move into the present, they must clear the past. Walking around with old resentment is like walking around carrying a heavy backpack. It burdens you. It's hard to be happy living under these constraints. Let it go.

Find Joy through Pain, Misery and Loss

There may be terrible things we experience in our lifetimes, such as war or death. We need an appropriate length of time to mourn before we can return to joy – not to cover up the tragedy, but to lighten our load through laughter.

I remember attending a funeral as a child of a distant, elderly relative. Several of the people were laughing after the funeral service and I thought it was horrible. Someone had *died* and people were having *fun*! I wondered if the next of kin would have a heart attack or a stroke overhearing this blatant act of disrespect.

And then I realized the next of kin was laughing the hardest of all.

There is a time to honor sadness and pain. Sit with it. Cry. Scream. Beat your fists into pillows. Breathe. Be silent. Allow yourself the time you need to heal. And allow yourself permission to be depressed. Many people are even scared to share their depression with close friends and family members. Some people take great pride in never letting anyone see them cry. Others want to comfort people in any way possible to avoid seeing someone sad.

Many societies are quick to medicate people who are depressed. For some, medication may help. For others, it may not. Every case is individual. What is universal about sadness and depression is that these are feelings that need to be honored as much as joy and anger. It's difficult to move past something when you deny that you're experiencing it. Give yourself time to sit with your depression. Bring joy into your life again when you're ready.

8

Forward-Thinking Scoundrel

Forward-Thinking Scoundrels are rarely in the present moment, which is the most serene, authentic and joyful moment we can experience. They tend to be people who are anxious and filled with doubt and worry. Forward-Thinking Scoundrels may live their life with a sense of urgency, moving from one thought or one task to the next without pause. They have little patience and want everything to be done "right now." Because of this urgency, they usually end up doing everything themselves.

Conversations tend to be extremely short because Forward Thinkers are already ahead of the current topic and realizing the sense of urgency for the next step in their day. However, some conversations may be extraordinarily long if the Forward Thinkers talk out their entire thought pattern as though they are writing a journal entry. They typically multi-task – their bodies moving almost as swiftly through the day as their minds. Confident Forward-Thinking Scoundrels tend to accomplish a great deal, while anxious Forward-Thinking Scoundrels tend to wallow in worry and have a difficult time beginning (or completing) projects.

Physical or mental burn-out is common in the lives of Forward-Thinking Scoundrels. Athletes who overtrain by not allowing themselves enough recovery time are at a greater risk of injury and illness. Likewise, placing too much stress on ourselves physically and mentally moves us into a stage of chronic exhaustion where autoimmune disorders, digestive, circulatory and endocrine problems can occur.

Financial health usually soars for Forward-Thinking Scoundrels until there is a health issue requiring time away from work, or back peddling to fix serious mistakes made while multi-tasking.

Spiritual health, however, tends to suffer as do relationships for Forward-Thinking Scoundrels. Emotional issues such as anxiety and nervous breakdowns can occur. Mental issues such as impaired focus, attention deficit and memory loss can also occur. Any one of these problems can shorten our life spans and/or decrease the quality of our lives. It is therefore paramount to our health, and our joy, to release Forward-Thinking Scoundrels from our lives.

The worst time for Forward-Thinking Scoundrels is bedtime. If they are unable to fall asleep, many Forward-Thinking Scoundrels become anxious and dwell on what they will need to do the next day. The lethargic feeling that accompanies sleep deprivation may help them to slow down their minds and actions initially, but long term it has disastrous effects.

True happiness comes to Forward-Thinking Scoundrels when they allow themselves time to rest, such as in the evening or when they are on vacation. These relaxing periods often occur after huge bouts of productivity. Even at these times, they may still be forward-thinking, but it is much less intense than is typical for them. Forward-Thinking Scoundrels also gain happiness when they reflect on past achievements and successes.

Slowing down is the best pathway to joy for Forward-Thinking Scoundrels. Scheduling less each day with more time between activities is helpful. Meditating, or deep breathing, will slow down the mind and will result in becoming more efficient and less harried. Short meditation periods, such as three minutes or less, done several times throughout the day will greatly calm these scoundrels and provide tranquility and contentment.

Comments you might hear from Forward-Thinking Scoundrels:

"I've only got a minute."
"I'm in a hurry."
"If only I had more time."
"I've got to remember to get bread at the grocery store and call Tom about baseball and..."
"Tomorrow will be too late. This needs to be taken care of ASAP."

If you OBSERVE and VERIFY the Forward-Thinking Scoundrel in your life, EXAMINE the following:

1. How has the Forward-Thinking Scoundrel helped you?
2. How has it negatively affected you?
3. To the best of your recollection, when were you first introduced to the Forward-Thinking Scoundrel? Is this a family, cultural or societal scoundrel you consciously or unconsciously accepted as your own?
4. What are some examples of how you've been a Forward-Thinking Scoundrel in the past week?
5. On a scale of one to ten, ten being the best, how would you rate your overall level of satisfaction and happiness in life?
6. In your circle, who else is visited by Forward-Thinking Scoundrels? Do you feel more harried around them?
7. From this moment onward, recognize when you are forward-thinking. Why are you doing it? Are you bored? Are you anxious?
8. How can you make your life more ideal? What is one thing you can do TODAY?

RELEASE Forward-Thinking Scoundrel Mentality with the following Affirmations:

- ॐ *All is right in my world.*
- ॐ *I am safe and protected.*
- ॐ *I am safe in the present moment.*
- ॐ *Everyone I know is safe and protected.*
- ॐ *I now choose to release all doubt.*
- ॐ *I trust in the Universe.*
- ॐ *I am in harmony with the Universe's schedule.*
- ॐ *Everything has a divine time and place.*
- ॐ *All good things will come to me in a divine timeline.*
- ॐ *I recognize realistic time frames, remaining calm and peaceful.*
- ॐ *I breathe deeply and become calm.*
- ॐ *I have the time, energy and ability to accomplish all that I need to accomplish.*
- ॐ *Breathing and meditating help me to become clear and focused.*
- ॐ *By focusing on my breathing rhythm, I still my mind and my thoughts.*

Be Present

Stressful emotions, such as anxiety, fear and depression instinctually cause a fight or flight reaction. A healthy example of a "fight" reaction is speaking your truth. A healthy reaction to a "flight" reaction would be to physically remove yourself from a situation to gain a different perspective. This could be done by taking a walk outdoors and getting fresh air.

What usually happens during a stressful situation, however, is much different. Instead of speaking their truth calmly, people tend to shout and rant. Instead of going outside, people tend to walk to the cookie jar, candy dish or coffee pot. Short-term, the kitchen journey and the yelling is immediately rewarding, but the long-term consequences are not favorable.

The quickest, easiest and most rewarding solution to decreasing levels of perceived stress is to live in a present state of awareness. This is accomplished through meditation, deep breathing and being conscious. You can do this in your immediate environment or outside of it. Shut your eyes to avoid extra mental stimulation. Take a long, deep breath through the nostrils allowing your belly and chest to rise. When you have pulled in as much oxygen as you can, exhale. Do not hold your breath at the top of the inhale nor at the bottom of the exhale. Allow your breath to be flowing and full. Focus on the inhale. Relax with the exhale.

Do a quick body scan. Do you have a headache? Imagine someone's fingers caressing your forehead. Feel your forehead and eyes relax. Is your jaw tense? Is your tongue pressed against the roof of your mouth? Slightly open your mouth. Allow your tongue to drop. Are your shoulders hunched? Does the back of your neck hurt? Roll your shoulder blades together, opening your chest. Lower your shoulders away from your ears.

Release your chin to one shoulder. Exhale and allow the stress to flow from your neck and shoulders. Bring your chin to the opposite shoulder and exhale again. Continue this mental scan, breathing and releasing tension in your body. Pay special attention to your hands, abdomen, lower back and feet. Then simply breathe.

Allow your thoughts to slow by focusing on your breathing. Let go of distractions inside your mind and around you. Acknowledge and release any new thoughts that crop into your mind. Looking to the past, we can feel angry, guilty, ashamed, embarrassed and depressed. Looking to the future, we can be anxious, worried and afraid. In the present moment, we are safe and all is well.

Inhale and exhale. Breathe in positive, creative energy. Exhale and release any negative, stale thoughts. Inhale peace and love. Exhale and let go of any doubt, worry or sadness.

There are many different ways to meditate. The right one is the one that works for you and the one that you *actually* do. Meditating with the breath is the quickest way for the mind and body to integrate with the soul. It is an opportunity for the Universe to communicate with us. It is an opportunity to listen instead of letting our Forward-Thinking Scoundrels chatter endlessly to ourselves. We can receive clear directions and clear answers during meditation.

A few deep breaths can alter the pH level of the blood, lower blood pressure, and balance the energy within the body. The more our breath is liberated, the less we are affected by trauma. We can inhale energy and suddenly renew our outlook on the stressful situation that occurred minutes ago. Not only is it now a possibility to deal with the situation, we may have also gained a new solution on how we can resolve it.

In moments of self-doubt, we can turn inward through meditation and deep breathing and gain the self-assurance we need for any feat we may attempt. This helps us to be present and also veers us away from potentially self-destructive methods of escape, such as unconscious eating, drinking, smoking, etc. It offers us a few precious moments during the day to rejuvenate ourselves and relax, which will give us a more optimistic outlook on ourselves and our environment.

Staying present makes us pay attention to when we are not mindful of potential danger. We may be likely to carry a heavy bag on one shoulder a long way if we are distracted. This could result in stiffness and pain. We may not notice a hole in the ground or misjudge walking around a desk. It allows us to correct bad habits and establish good ones.

By being mindful of the present moment, we release the past and the present and the whole realm of anxiety and regret that is exaggerated in our memory and our projections. The present moment nearly always finds us safe and protected. As long as our basic needs are met, the present moment is blissful. Our senses become alive in the present. We see and hear fine details, feel interesting textures, and savor familiar aromas and tastes. It opens channels of compassion and empathy toward other people. It helps us experience things more deeply and fully.

Slow Down

Many Forward-Thinking Scoundrels spend their days buzzing about from one activity to the next without being aware of anything they are doing. Sometimes Forward-Thinking Scoundrels find themselves doing two or three things at once while their brains are already engaged in the future. It would not be uncommon to find them driving, talking on a cell phone, fidgeting with music and planning their dinner during a pause in conversation. That's multi-tasking at its finest!

The problem with multi-tasking is that while Forward-Thinking Scoundrels think they are getting so many things accomplished, in reality they are only accomplishing many things poorly. They are being poor drivers by not paying full attention to the road. If a squirrel or a child were to dart out in front of the car, their reflexes would be slower because they are hampered by the other things they are doing. They're also being poor listeners since they're involved in so many other things instead of being fully present in the conversation. They are not honoring their bodies by paying attention to their nutritional needs. They would be better off simply driving, taking time later to check in with their bodies on what they need for dinner, eating dinner mindfully and then making their phone calls after dinner.

But Forward-Thinking Scoundrels tend to be in a frantic pace most of the day. This is the choice they have made, since each person is responsible for creating his or her reality and the pace in which that reality unfolds. They choose their commitments through their thoughts and actions. While they continue to move at such a rapid pace, they only allow more time for more things to fit into their schedules. It's an endless cycle.

In order to slow down the pace of our lives, we must actually *slow down*. When we slow down, fewer things will be able to fit in our lives. The things in which we engage then gain our full attention and become more enjoyable because we are more relaxed and less distracted.

The best time to begin to slow down your pace is during vacation. (This is also the best time to release your Fear of Happiness Scoundrel. See Chapter Four: Fear of Happiness Scoundrels: Never Ending Vacation.) Without normal commitments and routines to follow, you will be able to create a new agenda. Keep that agenda simple, especially on the first few days of vacation. Use your vacation as a rest or retreat. Sleep as much as you want. Soak in the bathtub. Sit and savor each bite of your meal. Be a sloth. Move as slowly and methodically as you can, becoming conscious of each and every movement. Take naps. Meditate. Go for long walks. Lie on the earth. Watch animals. Journal. Daydream.

Plan a maximum of one or two endeavors each day. Don't feel obligated to visit every tourist spot. Plan to go to a place that has no travel guide and nothing much to see or do. Choose the place by blindly picking a spot on a map. Or by the climate. Or because it has a nice hiking trail or a beautiful beach. Move through your day with ease. Stop multi-tasking. There is no need to multi-task because you are creating a simple agenda. If you are traveling with others, you can make a compromise between following your agenda for a few days and following theirs for a few days. Agree to a day or more apart from each other, each following a separate agenda.

Make your travel arrangements so that you can have a day or two at home following your vacation. Again, create your agenda so that you have few, if any, mandatory priorities. Use this time to transition into your regular life, while maintaining the slow and conscious pace to which you've become accustomed. Bring the harmony you found on vacation into your home and into your life.

When you return to a more regular schedule, continue to apply these principles of living gracefully. Forget your former harried lifestyle. Stop overbooking and under resting. Figure out what your passions are in life. If you are contemplating adding to your schedule, check to make sure everything aligns with your passions.

You don't need to do everything that comes your way. Learn to say no to things that will add stress or complicate your life. Keep life simple. Meditate on whether accepting the opportunity is best for the highest good. Meditate on whether it aligns with your higher purpose and your divine plan. Allow your intuition, your heart and your higher power to guide you to the right answer.

Unless you have absolute clarity and certainty that you should immediately accept an offer, wait to respond. Do not place urgency on other people's needs or desires, or on your own. Take your time and flow with a divine pace. Just as much as we don't need to be overwhelmed with tasks in our lives, neither do we need to be overwhelmed with opportunities or commitments. Think about what things you really *want* to commit to. Give yourself some time, perhaps a day, before you agree to *do* anything. The twenty-four-hour rule works well. Before agreeing to any invitation, offer or opportunity, tell the person you'll take a look at your schedule. Or say you'll see how you feel at the time of the event, without making any commitment. Keep things open so you can stay in the present moment and allow your body and spirit to make the decision, rather than your forward-thinking mind. Be flexible with the twenty-four-hour rule and allow that same flexibility to apply on the day of an event. The idea behind the twenty-four-hour rule is to avoid the twenty-four-hour regret. Avoid impulsive agreements. Obligations and excuses become unnecessary, if you stay uncommitted to things.

Check in with the pace of your present lifestyle. How can you establish a slower rhythm in your day? Do you take breaks? Take the opportunity for a break right now. Take a few deep breaths. Close your eyes and get calm. Relax. Lower your head down into a forward folding position, such as resting your head on your desk or lap. Forward folds bring calming energy into the body.

By taking several breaks throughout the day, you will be calmer and more efficient. It is a beautiful paradox that by slowing down, you become more productive. You gain greater clarity and focus by taking breaks. If you are at a computer for long periods of time, breaks become even more important to prevent eye strain. Rub your hands together to bring heat and healing energy into your palms and gently cup your hands over your eyes. Palming your eyes in this fashion is a phenomenal method to completely rest the facial and eye muscles and receive all the other benefits of taking a break.

The amazing pace Forward-Thinking Scoundrels move at is perfectly fine, as long as that speed allows for gracefulness and ease. If it doesn't, then it's time to slow down your pace. Find a pace that is relaxed. With breaks you gain greater efficiency. By removing superfluous tasks from your life, you gain time. Make sure all that you are tending to is aligned with your chosen path. If you still find there's too much on your plate to eliminate a hectic, harried lifestyle, delegate your tasks to your partner, co-worker, friend or child.

The more activities we try to squeeze into our day, the more irritable we become. How joyful can we be when we rush from one activity to the next without transitioning or enjoying ourselves? Imagine a day in the life of a cat. It wakes up when it's hungry, eats and saunters about its space, allowing whatever captivates its attention to be its total focus for a few minutes. It continues to stroll, stretches when it needs to, grooms itself uninhibitedly and eventually finds a sunny spot to take a nap. There isn't much need to busy itself with anything at all. It finds its contentment through its basic needs and sunny siestas.

Can you imagine spending day after day like a cat with no books, televisions, computers, cars or work? If someone supported you, fed you and cleaned up after you, how long would you be able to do nothing and enjoy it?

The idea seems ridiculous, doesn't it? We can't really compare our lives to that of a cat's, can we?

In the big scheme of things, however, who wouldn't like to curl up in the middle of the day and take a nap? If it's appropriate for animals, why isn't it appropriate for us? There aren't too many chronically stressed cats. But there are millions of stressed adults walking around every day.

Why do we allow this stress in our bodies and our minds? Why do we allow it in our faces? How do we eliminate it?

The first step to removing stress from your life is to get present by slowing down. Weigh every single action in your day with two questions:

1. Is it absolutely mandatory that I do this activity?
2. Is this activity going to bring me more peace and joy?

A negative response to either question gives you your answer. However, it does not necessarily mean that you should not do your activity, if not doing it will create greater consequences and stress for you than doing it. But be aware that you don't enjoy the activity. Consider altering the activity in some way. If the activity is not able to be altered, change your perception of it.

Next, examine the negative aspects of the activity. Exactly what is it about the activity that you don't like? How can you change these aspects? Be open to any and all possibilities, even those you may not recognize at present. Alter your perception of the unchangeable negative qualities in the activity. Find a positive spin for them. For example, if you hate correcting other people's mistakes, be glad there aren't more mistakes. Gratitude can clear a great deal of negativity.

Remember to slow down and to relax. The slower and more conscious you become, the more effortless your life will be.

Relax

Being present and slowing down help to bring us to a state of relaxation. To move into this state, find moments in your life when you can carve out pockets of time to devote to absolutely nothing. Extend the duration of those times. Make a game out of it. See how long you can simply *be* and not *do*. Make it a point to relax through meditation, napping or deep breathing. Do not watch television, read or do anything else. Be still. Imagine and trust that you have endless amounts of time to relax. Release all sense of urgency from your life. If you believe that you are strapped for time, re-examine your priorities. Recognize what is truly important and determine how to be efficient at completing these tasks. View relaxing, meditating and sleeping as the three most important tasks in your day. By doing these three activities, you will decrease stress and increase your efficiency and productivity. They will help you be more peaceful and pleasant. They will bring clarity to your life.

Sometimes we hold too tightly onto our agendas. We place importance on things that are less significant than taking breaks. We also have an amazing ability to fill blocks of time with seemingly trivial acts. For example, our souls may be screaming at us to lie down and nap during a cleaning frenzy, but we avoid it. Or we see a beautiful overlook while on a bike ride yet we propel our bodies onward.

Forward-Thinking Scoundrels continuously fritter away their time. They move about unconsciously, without breaks. What happens in these situations is that the mind and the body, especially the nervous system, go into overdrive causing edginess and manic behaviors. Breakdown and burnout are close at hand.

A switch in perception needs to occur. Value and importance need to be placed on relaxation. What good is a clean house if you have exhausted yourself to get it clean? What good is a manicured lawn if your back is wrought with tension because you avoided taking a break? What good is accomplishing loads of computer work if your eyes are strained and your shoulders and chest are tight from hovering over the keyboard for hours?

Time spent in relaxation lets the body, mind and spirit become harmonious and recover from the hundreds of tasks we demand of ourselves.

Sit still. Relax. Enjoy.

Be.

Sleep

In this technological age, we have become a society so "advanced" that we have forgotten to fulfill our basic needs and we have sought technology to return us to a state of proper health.

Sleep is an important component to a healthy lifestyle and therefore it is a component to living a life full of joy. Unfortunately, in today's fast-paced, time-starved society, it is often overlooked. Many people tend to push it aside in favor of finishing paperwork, housework, watching television, using the computer or socializing. But missing out on valuable hours of sleep can have enormous repercussions in life.

Sleep allows the body to recharge itself. During this time, skin wastes are eliminated. Minerals, vitamins and hormones are circulated. While sleeping, your body produces infection-fighting substances. Muscle adaptation and growth occur during this crucial recovery time. Many correlations are being found between sleep deprivation and negative health impacts, such as hypertension, diabetes, obesity, memory loss and decreased metabolic rates. Getting adequate sleep can make an enormous difference in your daily routine, your workouts, your perspective on life and the way you handle stress. If you do not get enough sleep:

- you will look to food or caffeine for energy.
- food choices will often be processed food – high in sugar and carbohydrates and low in nutritional value.
- any exercise program you engage in will be less intense and less enjoyable.
- you may skip one or several workouts because you lack energy.

People who are sleep deprived tend to be less efficient at work and at home. They have less energy. People who do not get adequate sleep may be more irritable, depressed and accident-prone. Mood shifts can occur more easily when someone is sleep deprived. It is a challenge to be content in your life when you are not getting enough sleep.

How much sleep you need is dependent on several factors. Rather than a set number of hours, such as eight or nine, it is more important to look at some signs that can tell you if you need more sleep:

- you have trouble remembering or concentrating.
- you depend on an alarm clock.
- you hit the snooze button.
- you fall asleep sitting in meetings or traffic.
- you struggle to get out of bed in the morning.
- you sleep late on weekends.

If any of the above signs are true for you, it's time to make sleep a priority in your life. Make an effort to get to bed earlier at night. Think about everything you do from the time you leave work to the time you go to bed at night. Avoid or minimize watching television or using the Internet. Postpone activities that can wait until the weekend.

In the morning, eliminate any activities that can be done later in the day. Some things we do for the sake of our vanity may actually be stealing away precious minutes of our beauty sleep.

Go to sleep and wake up at the same time every day, including the weekend. Eliminate noises or lights that disrupt your sleep. If you have trouble falling asleep, try a hot bath or meditation. Avoid exercise or eating before bedtime as both activities stimulate your body.

On days that you do not get enough sleep, take a nap. Although naps are not proven to be as effective as a full night's sleep, they will counter some of the negative effects of sleep deprivation. Meditation will also help.

Prioritize

Most of us have at least one thing that we've been putting off because we don't want to do it. We lack motivation. Perhaps there is a perceived (or real) lack of time. It may be something we've put off for a few weeks, months, years or decades. Unless there is a deadline to motivate us, our unfinished business occupies the bottom spot on our priority list. But the horrible thing is that it does not leave the list. It holds on for dear life at the bottom of that list and we stubbornly allow it to stay, just like our scoundrels.

And even though it's ever present on our to do lists, we still don't do it.

And the reason we don't do it is because we have no desire to do it.

It's likely the very last thing we want to do. But the unfortunate thing is that we feel guilty every time we think about it. It nags at us when we relax, reminding us that no matter how much we do and how much we have accomplished, we still have that last "project" to complete.

There are two different types of these bottom rung priorities. They are either a conclusive project or an ongoing one. The conclusive project is a bit easier to tackle. Once it's done, it's done. Fixing a door is a conclusive project. Keeping a closet organized is an ongoing project. Ongoing projects tend to be more intensive because they will need continual attention. Quitting an addiction, such as smoking, would belong to this category. Sticking to a healthy diet and exercise program would also be ongoing. These types of "projects" will get easier over time, but they are lifelong commitments. Therefore, they tend to be very psychologically demanding. The best way to view these tasks is to see that you can be victorious at them every single day. Every night you can go to bed a champion because you accomplished that difficult task.

But how do you find the motivation to begin? And once you begin, how do you become victorious? Thirdly, how do you make the one task you absolutely do not want to do enjoyable?

First of all, you must have a desire to do it. Do not approach this task with the mentality that *I should do this because...* Living in joy means throwing the word *should* out of your vocabulary. There is no joy in should. There is joy in the words: *I want to do this because...* Joy comes from taking control of your life by doing what you want to be doing. Until you are seriously ready to find that joy, leave the task at the bottom of the list. Find joy in letting it be there. Accept that it's there and that it will be dealt with in its right time. Release your guilt that you are not ready to tackle it now. There are emotional, spiritual and mental blocks that come along with physical tasks that we can't bring ourselves to accomplish. If we're not ready to uncover those issues, it's best to leave the task for its right timing.

Even though we claim to be too busy to take on anything new, there will always be time to squeeze in what we truly want to squeeze in. A top priority will find its way to completion if it's a true priority. Whatever tasks we avoid making a priority remain incomplete until they are made a priority by us or someone else. However, those tasks with unrecognized priorities leave us feeling defeated.

We are left with the feeling that we are not good enough because we cannot complete everything we think we should complete. However, since we have not set aside an exact day or time or an exact deadline, we have not set ourselves up for success. We are unconsciously sabotaging ourselves.

Do we want to perpetuate our unhappiness because we believe we're not good enough? Does anyone want to wake up every morning and go to sleep every night feeling overwhelmed by those unfinished tasks?

Of course not.

Affirm to yourself: *I am good enough. I do enough.*

When you have a few hours to devote to your projects, take a look at what remains unfinished in your life. Write everything on a sheet of paper – from dusting the living room to getting an oil change to finding Aunt Mildred a birthday present. Then choose five of these tasks as your top priorities. How many of those five tasks can you complete today? Be realistic on this so you can be successful. You'll feel better if you complete three chosen tasks than choose all five tasks and complete three. Write the tasks you can realistically complete today on a separate sheet of paper. Anything not written on this paper is no longer a main concern for you. Mentally discard the first list.

Now, focus on your list. Make a promise to yourself that you will complete this list. Begin and complete the first task. Stay present with that task and don't begin the second task until the first is completed unless there is a waiting time on the task. For instance, if you are waiting for laundry to be clean or food to marinate or an oil change, then move on to the next task.

If you need help with something, call a friend or a professional and get help. If you lack motivation for a task, incorporate a reward or something fun, such as a movie afterward. One simple and effective reward system is called: The Gift Box. The Gift Box gives you a visual and tangible reward for your efforts. It reminds you as you are going through the steps to reach your goal that there is an extra magical surprise waiting for you. The Gift Box lets you know that someone cares about you and wants to see you be successful. Even if you decide to create The Gift Box for yourself, you will be spending the time to do something special for yourself.

When there is something that you want a child to do, such as a household chore, and the child refuses to do it, you have many options, two of which are to establish a punishment or a reward.

If you decide you'll try the reward system, you can package your reward inside of the biggest box you can find and tie a red ribbon on the box. Placing it in the middle of the living room floor, you tell the child that when the chore is finished, the box can be opened.

Now unless the child is stubborn or has reason to doubt that you have placed a suitable reward in the Gift Box, the child will be curious enough to do the chore and earn the reward. Who wouldn't be enticed into doing their chores if they knew a giant box with a red ribbon was waiting on the other end?

As adults, we need to honor the little child inside of us. Fun surprises for difficult tasks are what make life joyous. And not only is the task that you've dreaded now complete, but you earned a fun little reward as well.

"Jessica" wanted her husband to join her Saturday yoga class because he had been complaining of lower back pain for months and she knew that yoga would help his back. Although there were other males in the class, including one of his good friends, he was reluctant to join. Jessica bought two tickets to a concert he had wanted to go to inside a box and placed it on the dining room table, announcing that he would get to open The Gift Box after yoga class. With the extra incentive, he finally agreed to try her yoga class and he loved it (and the concert tickets). He continued on with the yoga class even after his friend had dropped out, which helped him gain flexibility and decrease his lower back pain. The Gift Box had also helped to strengthen their marriage, knowing how much his wife cared about him to encourage him to do yoga.

There does not have to be a dollar value attached to The Gift Box. The idea behind it is to offer a fun reward to someone we care about to acknowledge them for a job well done. The Gift Box is also set up for accountability. All of a sudden that task we've been putting off for years now gets done because there is a fun, little reward waiting for us at the end.

Discover what patterns work for you. Be disciplined and genuine with yourself. If you find yourself distracted or quitting before your list is complete, get back on track! That was the promise you made. Also, don't allow non-priorities to sneak in and steal away time from your true priorities. Remember, the affirmation: *I do enough*. The goal is to eliminate non-prioritized tasks. If it wasn't important enough to get on your original list, it's not important. Unless it's something absolutely critical, such as an emergency surgery or a broken down automobile, it's a non-priority.

"Omar" had stacks of papers in a kitchen cupboard that needed to be filed. He also had an empty file cabinet in an upstairs closet. He recognized that if he spent a few hours, he could organize the cabinet. The peace of mind from accomplishing the task would be high. And he could rid himself of any subconscious guilt he had over his lack of motivation to complete the task. Omar had an exact idea of how he wanted the papers sorted. He had the file folders he needed to organize the papers. And he had the file cabinet sitting empty.

Yet he didn't sort the papers.

And the reason he didn't sort the papers is because he didn't have a desire to sort them. The papers were his symbolic padding. They were his protection from the world. At one point in his life, many of the same papers had been in stacks around his bed. They served as padding and protection to keep away a serious, loving relationship, which he consciously wanted and subconsciously feared.

When he finally realized the symbolism of the papers in his life, he found the desire to organize the cabinet. Omar asked for help from a friend. Together, they recycled thousands of papers. They organized papers into folders and put the folders in the file cabinet that had sat empty for more than a year. He went to bed that night with a new sense of freedom.

The next day, Omar had two amazing connections with acquaintances he had met a few months earlier. They were two people he had been ready to receive into his life because he had torn down his physical barrier. Other new people filtered into his life and his circle of friends expanded. The depth of his relationships increased. When the papers were eliminated, the energetic barrier was also lifted. He released the fear he had been carrying. The false need Omar had to protect himself dissolved. He allowed a thousand new layers of joy into his life because he released the thousands of papers that were holding him back.

After the last of your tasks is complete, be aware of the synchronicity that occurs because you completed tasks that were energetically suffocating you. Celebrate your success.

Analyze Your Goals

Many people set futuristic, idealistic goals for themselves. Goal setting can be a very powerful and positive thing. Attaining your goals is even more wonderful. However, sometimes we need to ask ourselves why we are setting certain goals. Do we really want to accomplish that goal? Do we need to accomplish the goal? How will it enhance our lives when we accomplish the goal? Will it make us happier?

Or is it our family, our peers or our society that has set certain standards that we have decided to consciously or unconsciously adopt?

For instance, imagine that the majority of society is in awe of a certain car, which you also admire. Do you want the car because it has certain attributes you love or do you simply want it because everybody else wants it? The more people focus their energy on attaining that particular car, the more people will want that car.

Let's imagine this car to be a BMW. It doesn't matter what model, year, color, etc., you only dream of attaining a BMW. Begin by asking yourself why you want the BMW. Is it for the prestige of owning the car? Is it because your parents or friends have BMWs? Is it because you like the sporty look and heard they are reliable? Is it because when you were a young child, you read a story about a BMW and you have experienced hundreds of synchronistic events involving BMWs that have led you to believe that this make of automobile is perfect for you?

Once you establish why you have the goal, ask yourself how it will enhance your life. Will it make you healthier? Smarter? Stronger? What new characteristics will you have or hone when you attain your goal?

Ask yourself if your goal will make you happier. Will you be sacrificing more peace and happiness from your current lifestyle in order to attain your goal? Be honest in answering this question. We can fool ourselves into believing that owning a new car or house or boat will bring us ultimate happiness; but in reality, owning any of these may not bring us much more joy at all. For example, the boat may be fun for the first summer and then insurance, gas, storage, docking fees and maintenance costs may far outweigh our fun with the boat. All of a sudden our toy has become a nightmare and we wish we had never bought the boat in the first place. Sometimes we refuse to see all the details until we are actually in the situation. But it may be too late at that point.

That is why it is necessary to answer the question: Will attaining your goal truly make you happier?

Goals and dreams can give our lives purpose. But make your goals individual to you and know why you have chosen your goals. If there is a goal you set ten years ago that remains unfulfilled and you no longer feel the passion that you did when you originally wrote the goal, eliminate it. When goals no longer fit who you are and what you want, you don't need those goals. It's better to release them than to manifest them into reality and be miserable.

In summary, the four questions you can ask yourself in goal setting are:

- Why did I set this goal for myself?
- What is the purpose of this goal?
- How will attaining this goal enhance my life?
- Will attaining this goal truly make my life happier?

By asking yourself these four questions, you can get rid of unnecessary goals and unnecessary pressure you may be putting on yourself, leaving room for happiness and fun.

9
Grass is Greener Scoundrel

The Grass is Greener Scoundrels look beyond their talents, possessions and status. They see something outside of themselves that someone else possesses and they desire it, believing that if they, too, had that "thing," they would be happier and more fulfilled. It may be something as simple as their neighbor's garden or as complex as their friend's spouse or new baby. They are filled with envy and jealousy.

They typically lack confidence in themselves and their abilities and lack joy in their lives. Instead, they focus on the things they don't have.

The Grass is Greener Scoundrels are not seeing their lives with eyes of gratitude. They are stuck in sibling rivalry behavior, having been compared to or having compared themselves to their brothers, sisters or other peers. Grass is Greener Scoundrels may even look at two similarly filled glasses and consider theirs half empty and the other person's glass half full. The competitive nature of these scoundrels comes out in many of the roles they play in life. As parents, they want the best for their children and they expect the best from their children. As leaders, they have high expectations of their projects and staff. High expectations can be helpful for their end results, but continuous comparisons along the way can be frustrating. The internal turmoil Grass is Greener Scoundrels face in their drive to stay ahead of the competition is personally felt by everyone in their lives.

They are happiest when they attain something they have been coveting or when they are able to forget what it is they desire. This happiness, however, is fleeting. Soon enough, there will be something else they want. Searching for happiness outside of themselves will always keep them searching. With a core belief that the grass is greener elsewhere, they will never attain authentic, lasting happiness.

The root of their unhappiness lies in their lack of self-love and self-acceptance. Making a list of gratitude will internalize their focus on the abundance in their lives, rather than focus on a perceived "lack." It becomes much harder to be envious of your cousin's new puppy when you recognize your gratitude for your faithful, old greyhound. Trusting in the Universe that we are supported and have all that we need, we no longer need to look outside of ourselves.

Comments you might hear from Grass is Greener Scoundrels:

"I want a speed boat just like the Nelsons'."
"It sure would be nice to have straight hair."
"I would love to live in the mountains instead of living by the ocean."
"Aw, why didn't I get picked for that assignment?"
"I wish I had been able to do that. He's so lucky."

If you OBSERVE and VERIFY the Grass is Greener Scoundrel in your life, EXAMINE the following:

1. How has the Grass is Greener Scoundrel helped you?
2. How has it negatively affected you?
3. To the best of your recollection, when were you first introduced to the Grass is Greener Scoundrel? Is this a family, cultural or societal scoundrel you consciously or unconsciously accepted as your own?
4. What are some examples of how you've been a Grass is Greener Scoundrel in the past week?
5. On a scale of one to ten, ten being the best, how would you rate your overall level of satisfaction and happiness in life?
6. In your circle, who else is visited by the Grass is Greener

Scoundrels? With whom do you find yourself commiserating about what you want?

7. From this moment onward, recognize when you are focusing on greener grass elsewhere. In what ways do you think you would be happier if you got what you desire? In what ways would you be at a disadvantage? How long would you estimate staying happy?

8. How can you make your life more ideal? What is one thing you can do TODAY?

RELEASE Grass is Greener Scoundrel Mentality with the following Affirmations:

- ॐ *I am enough.*
- ॐ *I have enough.*
- ॐ *I do enough.*
- ॐ *I have all that I need right now.*
- ॐ *The greatest things I possess are my health and happiness.*
- ॐ *I am perfect as I am now.*
- ॐ *The Universe provides me with all that I need and desire.*
- ॐ *I find happiness within myself.*
- ॐ *I accept and approve of myself.*
- ॐ *I am grateful for all I have received and all that is being prepared for me.*
- ॐ *I am satisfied.*

Recognize the Perfection in Your Life

"Bill" never cared much about owning or driving a car. There have been many years where Bill did not need a car at all. He loves the freedom of walking or biking everywhere and he still does this the majority of the time. For the moment, however, it is necessary for him to own a car and drive it occasionally to appointments. He owns a red Honda that he bought used with thirty-thousand miles on it. It is not fancy by any means, but Bill considers it his dream car. No one has ever pulled alongside him at a stop light to admire his Honda and yet it is still his dream car. Why? Because it runs perfectly, it's clean and it's paid in full. It is not sporty or stylish. It was not even made in the twenty-first century. And yet it is Bill's dream car because he owns it and he loves it.

What else might your society not consider remarkable, but for you it's perfect and ideal? You may likely realize that there are many aspects of your life that are already perfect; you just haven't recognized them yet. Make sure you're not settling or being complacent about anything in your life. Instead recognize the magic and perfection that already exists. Express your gratitude for your good fortune.

Look at your living space and determine what needs to be done to it to make it ideal. If you live in an apartment and you would rather be in a house or cabin, there may be nothing you can do about that right this moment. Visualize your ideal living space and believe that it will manifest in its own perfect timing. In the meantime, make alterations in your current living quarters. What needs to be done to make it ideal?

Get fresh flowers, plants and a few bright pillows or paintings to redecorate the area. Make changes in individual rooms until each room is ideal for you. Create your dream master bedroom, your dream living room, dining room, etc. Nurture each room with your time and love, to create better peace of mind, clarity, creativity and happiness in your life. Reassess how the space looks and feels.

If your living space is cluttered, spend some time cleaning it. If your work space is scattered with papers, organize it. Ask someone to help you if you aren't enthusiastic about doing it. There are interior designers, feng shui practitioners, professional organizers and house cleaners who specialize in this. Enlist their help. Tiny enhancements in your space can make huge differences – whether you are conscious of them or not.

By realizing the perfection you have manifested in your life, you can relax more. Because once you own your dream car, you no longer need to work to attain your dream car. By having the ideal social life, you no longer need to add more social activities into your schedule.

Look at different areas of your life as well, such as your spiritual life and physical life. Change any aspects of your life that you do not consider ideal or perfect.

Also be able to recognize the perfection in yourself, something Grass is Greener Scoundrels seldom do. When we are content in the present moment, we discover that we have all that we need. It will not matter if we own a sports car, a Honda or if we don't have any car at all. If we can recognize the perfection that we are alive and breathing, we can find the contentment and the joy in our lives.

Recognize the Beauty in Your Life

Just like a great piece of music elevates our mood, so does something beautiful. Surround yourself with beauty as often as possible. Beauty can be a subjective thing, so choose what you find beautiful and absorb yourself in its atmosphere. Find beauty with all of your senses. Watching a horse move is magical and that experience can be heightened by listening to it breathe or neigh. Listen to its tail swish and its hooves tap against the ground. Listen to the grasses flutter around it. Listen to other animals nearby – birds, dogs and chickens. Smell the flesh of the horse or the leather of its saddle. Touch its smooth coat, its coarse mane and tail. Feel the strength of its muscles, the softness of its nose. See the different hues in its hair. Experience the horse and its environment.

Flowers, the sunset, the sunrise, green grass, gardens, horses, sapphires, works of technological genius, handcrafted goods, textiles, insects, houses, cakes, cars, lakes – all of these conjure up different images for people. Some may find horses absolutely amazing and breathtaking while others find them scary and smelly. If it makes your heart light, immerse yourself in its presence. If it doesn't, avoid it.

If you live in a run-down neighborhood, do what you can to beautify it. Pick up garbage, fix what is broken or damaged, paint over graffiti and plant flowers. Ask your neighborhood association or city council members for help in doing this. If you live in the city, spend time in nature or bring nature into your space.

Soak in the beauty of the present moment and your surroundings. Do not focus on beauty that is external to your reality. Trust that beauty is abundant for you. Recognize and revel in it.

Realize the Beauty and Strength of Your Physical Body

It is fairly easy for most people to realize the strength of their bodies. Our kidneys and lungs are amazingly strong and resilient, and so are our lymphatic systems, endocrine systems and immune systems. But most people, especially Grass is Greener Scoundrels, struggle with accepting their external physical body in the present moment. Rather than focus on what they like about themselves, people focus on what they need to improve. Take a moment and think about two people whom you are close to who you would consider handsome or beautiful with nice physiques. If you were to ask them if they thought they had beautiful bodies, what do you think they would they say? What if you asked them to tell you what they would like to improve with their physical appearance? Would they give you a list of minor things they would like to change about themselves? Many people would.

Millions of people are employed because of this insecurity. The advertising industry, fashion industry and cosmetic industry, as well as plastic surgeons, are supported by this desire to improve ourselves from the outside.

It does not serve you to dislike any part of your body. It does not help you to hate your thighs. It does not improve your quality of life to have a smaller nose or bigger breasts. You will not be a better person in the world if you have fewer wrinkles.

So why do we continue to buy into society's game of hating the way we look?

In essence, this means hating what we see when we look into the mirror. Or at least wishing we were different in a few ways.

In junior high, "Kelly" became self-conscious of her tiny, non-existent chin. She especially hated her profile and believed that she was not pretty because she did not have a "normal" chin. She had sparkling green eyes, a beautiful smile and naturally curly hair, but because of her chin, she did not believe she was beautiful.

The summer before eighth grade, Kelly went to summer camp. Midway through the week, while playing Capture the Flag, a player from the opposing team accidentally hit Kelly's chin. It swelled profusely and when she went to the hospital a week later, x-rays showed her jaw was broken and needed to be reset through surgery.

To this day, Kelly's jaw is the only thing she has ever broken and the pain from breaking and resetting it was the worst she's ever encountered. Interesting that at the time, it was the only thing she hated, the only thing she didn't care enough to protect. Her chin could have served her better if she had cared about it more. Perhaps she would not have broken it. She is grateful that she did not grow up hating her ears or her eyes because she shudders to think what might have happened if she had damaged those.

Over time, Kelly learned to love her chin, and she learned to love every part of her body. This is a healthy, wonderful place where we can all be. There may be days where you question if you are getting deeper wrinkles or if your thighs are getting bigger, but love them anyway. After all, your thighs have done a wondrous amount of work for you, haven't they? They carry you up and down stairs and help you get out of bed every morning. Why shouldn't you love them? And what about your wrinkles? What benefits would you have in life without them? Be confident that your body is marvelous at any age and enjoy the respect you receive.

If instead you chose to hate your thighs, perhaps they would retaliate by storing cellulite. Perhaps your hamstring muscles would become tight. Maybe you would get varicose veins or you would bruise them often because you don't care about them. Or maybe none of these things would happen. Maybe your thighs would just hang out on your body, unbothered by your opinion of them. But your self-esteem and love for yourself will suffer. Likewise, you could try to fight wrinkles, but it is better to come to peace with them. Do not expend your strength by fighting a war with yourself. And stop spending time being envious of others who are beautiful or handsome. There are too many other important things to do.

"Susan" hired me as a personal trainer to help her lose weight after she had given birth to her first child. Four months later, she weighed two pounds less than she had before getting pregnant. Pleased with how she looked, Susan realized for the first time in her life how amazing her body was. She viewed it as amazing – not because she was thinner than she had been, but because it had given her the two most precious gifts she had – her health and her child. She remembers wishing in high school that she had smaller legs. Now, as an adult, her legs are bigger than at age sixteen, but she likes them better. More than anything, she doesn't want her daughter growing up thinking it's okay to hate her body.

Ideally, none of us want our children to hate themselves in any manner. What better way to teach them this, than to model it? Develop a healthy body image and refer to your body with loving, approving words.

To develop a positive body image, use the **OVER Technique** to liberate your former negative thoughts about your body. **Observe** (or visualize) yourself naked in a mirror. Identify what you don't like about yourself and then **verify** the things that you truly don't like, perhaps by remembering negative things you've thought or said. Write the body parts you dislike on a paper. If you can't name any, that's fantastic – as long as you are being totally honest with yourself. Can you name any parts you would change if you were granted the opportunity to change them? **Examine** why you dislike them. What are the reasons you dislike them? Has anyone ever complimented you on them? How have they served you in life? How would you feel if something terrible happened to them (i.e. they get broken, stabbed, bruised, infected with cancer)?

Release the negative thoughts about these body parts by focusing on positive aspects of each of the body parts you dislike. For example, if you dislike your freckled shoulders, maybe you have very good muscle tone on them. Or maybe you have great posture. If you dislike your belly, maybe you appreciate the fact that you never get cramps or stomach aches. Or that you always stay nice and warm in your torso region because you are well-insulated.

Once you have found some positive attributes about the things you dislike in your physical appearance, make a list of your favorite physical qualities. Spend time on every body part – your shoulders, fingers, ankles, neck, toes... Find reasons why you like them. How have they served you in life?

The human body was made divinely. It is beautiful and strong no matter what size or shape it is. Our parts fulfill many purposes. Take a moment and develop a healthy list that focuses on the parts you feel good about. Be creative in your reasoning.

Be Grateful

Be thankful for everything that comes your way – both the "good" and "bad." There are lessons in everything and you will find great benefits in your life from some of the worst situations you will ever face. Lessons you are meant to learn will manifest and reappear until you have learned the lesson.

The glass can be half full or half empty. It depends on your perception and your gratitude. You can be miserable knowing your vacation is half over or you can be grateful that you are on vacation. You can curse the airlines for delaying your flight three hours or you can be grateful that they're being cautious about foul weather. And then an hour into your wait, you can be grateful you have the opportunity to talk to the person next to you who has now become a contact for you at a company with which you recently applied for a job.

On New Year's Eve, "Beth" was spending the night at home with her family, all of whom were suffering from a cold, herself included. At only ten o'clock, her husband had fallen asleep as they were watching a movie. One of their twins woke up complaining about a diaper that needed changing, which in turn woke her husband.

When her husband returned from changing the diaper, Beth, eight months pregnant, grumbled that it was not exactly the glamorous evening of champagne and caviar they had three years earlier.

"Well, you can look at it that way," he said, rubbing her aching lower back, "or you can see it the way I do. I'm at home with my family whom I love very much. I was awakened by one of my rapidly growing children and got to spend a precious moment with him during the middle of the night. Now I'm back in our warm bed with my beautiful wife by my side. There's no amount of champagne or caviar that could make me happier."

Recognize the good fortune in any occurrence, and you will become grateful for all events in your life. In fact, the "bad" events will virtually disappear because your perception will have changed. There may still be flight delays and New Year's Eves with dirty diapers, but you will see the positive side of these events and be grateful for what they bring you. This gratitude, in turn, will reflect upon your good fortune. It will remind you of the good things in your life. The joy in your life will increase when you recognize what you can do or what you have done.

Being grateful can even be applied to activities you do not enjoy. When you find yourself bothered by having to brush your teeth, be grateful that you have healthy teeth and the ability to brush them.

At the age of sixteen, I became a certified nursing assistant at a nursing home. Day after day, I witnessed my patients' quality of life deteriorating before their deaths. I worked with people that couldn't bathe themselves, feed themselves or brush their teeth. Many of them couldn't remember their names.

This was not a happy atmosphere for a high school student. But it was in this dismal atmosphere that I quickly learned a great deal of gratitude. Instead of being depressed, I became grateful. I was grateful that my body was healthy and functioning properly. I was grateful that I could take care of myself and remember things. When my patients died, I was grateful that I had known them and had been able to help them in some manner. I was grateful that I had learned whatever I could from them.

Wherever you find yourself in life, recognize the goodness. Thank the Universe for all that you have received and for all that is being prepared for you. The more you express your gratitude, the more you will affirm your recognition of what you receive and the more accepting you will be to receive.

Be grateful for the little things as well as when your big dreams become fulfilled. Be grateful for each day, each breath, each glass of water and each smile. Be grateful for your family and your friends. Be grateful for those with whom you do not get along. They are your gurus. Discover what it is they are teaching you.

Be grateful for the winter and the spring, the summer and the fall. Be grateful for your health. In gratitude, accept what comes your way. Do not fight or allow friction with anything. Flow with grace and ease.

Be grateful for every bite of food you eat. Be grateful for Mother Earth, for the rich soil, the plants and the animals. Be grateful for simplicity, technology and harmony. Be grateful for the sun and moon and stars. For the power to change and the security in status quo. Be grateful for the reactionaries and the revolutionaries, the conformists and the leaders. Be grateful to what everyone brings to our world, whether or not you agree with them.

Be grateful for your journey.

Gratitude can change your perspective immediately. It is one of the simplest ways to become joyful because it takes you to a respectful mind-set where it's hard to complain about something in your life when you know there is someone else who would be lucky to be in your situation.

Spend a few moments and write a list of things for which you are grateful. It can be as simple as "I am grateful that the sun is shining today" or "I am grateful I am alive" to something more specific, such as "I am grateful for my home" or "I am grateful for my family." Read this list or make a new one whenever you feel that life is unfair or that you are not getting any breaks. Your list of gratitude will remind you that there are a lot of reasons in your life to be thankful. In many ways, you were born with a wealth of good fortune.

Nurture Yourself with Love

Grass is Greener Scoundrels harbor some degree of self-hatred. This could show up in any number of ways. Perhaps you get involved in unhealthy relationships. Maybe you have an unhealthy relationship to food or abuse drugs or alcohol. Maybe you criticize yourself. Maybe you are never satisfied with your appearance, continually making minor improvements to look more like someone you admire or like some imaginary ideal.

There are hundreds of other things you can do to act out your self-hatred. In some ways, they are easier to do than to love yourself. But ask yourself, would I rather spend my life loving myself or hating myself? Would I rather enjoy my life and enter into successful relationships and endeavors or would I rather hit dead ends? Would I rather have high self-esteem or low self-esteem? Would I rather be healthy and happy or miserable and in pain?

Once you recognize the patterns that perpetuate self-hatred, it becomes easier to love yourself. And once you truly love yourself, it is easier to love others and to create success and happiness in your life.

So, how do you begin to love yourself?

Use the same tool that you did to realize the beauty and strength of your physical body - the mirror. Look in the mirror, this time, it doesn't matter if you're naked, clothed, well-dressed or sloppy, if your hair is combed or not. Stare into your own eyes. Say, "I love you." Can you do it? Can you do it without conditions, such as allowing a thought to pop into your head afterward like: *I love you, but boy, those wrinkles are getting worse every day.* Or *I love you, but I've got to lose twenty pounds.* Or *I love you, but I don't love your gray hair.* Keep repeating the words "I love you" until no negative thoughts follow it. You need not get rid of your afterthoughts altogether, just change them to be more endearing. For example, *I love you and your wrinkles. I love you*

— every single pound of you. I love you and your lustrous gray hair.

It may seem ridiculous, but it is less ridiculous than continually shaming and belittling yourself. And it is far less ridiculous than shaming and belittling others. The more you learn to love every inch of yourself – outside and inside – the more you will be able to love others and to allow others to love you. As you become more loving and less critical with yourself, you will be less critical of others.

Looking in the mirror and saying you love yourself is a wonderful thing, but it is not the only way to show your love. Look at the way you take care of yourself. How much sleep are you getting? How much water do you drink? How many fruits and vegetables do you eat? How much of that is organic? Do you slow down during the day and allow yourself to relax? How often do you sit in the sunshine and breathe fresh air? Do you take vacations frequently? Do you enjoy time with friends? Do you laugh? Do you sing? How much do you enjoy life?

There are many things we can do each day to love ourselves. It's important to take the time we need to give ourselves that special attention, so that we can then spend our time showing other people how much we love them. Today, do something that shows how much you love yourself. Fairly similar to nurturing yourself with luxury, nurturing yourself with love can be a simple, completely free luxury. It could be going to bed early and getting nine hours of sleep. It could be making a nice cup of homemade cocoa and sitting down with a good book. It could be taking a long walk or bike ride. Honor yourself today in whatever loving ways you can. Release some of the rigid structure you have placed on yourself and do something loving.

As we begin to nurture ourselves with love, we will fall in love with ourselves and fall in love with life. We will stop looking at what other people have and stop envying them. We will find happiness and fulfillment inside of ourselves.

Release Competition

Do you enjoy competing? Do you enter into games, races or other circumstances where you can contend with others? What is it about competition that you enjoy? Do you like the title of champion? Do you like the recognition? Do you need the recognition to validate yourself and your talents?

"Heidi" was a competitive cyclist. Her self-esteem was high when it came to cycling – at least she thought it was high. It seemed to be high when she was winning. But she can remember earning second place at a race and thinking she was not really that good. Somehow Heidi had forgotten that she had won a dozen races so far that year and she would probably win another dozen before the end of the year. She also ignored the fact that there were hundreds of people still out racing the course after she had finished that would have gladly accepted second place. But she didn't recognize any of that. In that moment, she saw herself as a failure because she hadn't accomplished her goal for that day. Until she won another race, she would remain a failure.

This is not high self-esteem. It shows exactly how low her self-esteem was. Heidi constantly needed to reevaluate her worth through winning. Unless she won, she was a failure.

How many trophies and medals would it have taken Heidi to improve her self-esteem? She finally realized there was no amount of metal in the world that would help her think better about herself. She had to improve her self-worth in other ways. Competition with others was not the way to do it. Heidi had to realize independently from the races and the medals that she was a great cyclist *and* a great person.

To improve her self-esteem, she had to step away from racing for a while and seek other endeavors, so she took guitar lessons and a painting class. She tried kayaking, rock climbing and surfing. She spent more time in the kitchen testing new recipes. Heidi wanted to discover what things she liked rather than what she had always been programmed to do.

Heidi dabbled in races for a while longer, but she found more fulfillment and happiness outside of her cycling life. She realized there are other things she wanted to experience in her lifetime. Now she bikes for fun and for transportation and to give her body the opportunity to move in that familiar rhythm. She bikes to get fresh air, clear her mind and to clear out toxins from her body. And although she doesn't move nearly as fast or as far as she did, every day she knows she is a great cyclist because she *enjoys* it.

When you have happiness and a healthy self-esteem, you don't need to *do* anything to prove that you are a talented person. You are talented because you enjoy who you are and the things you do.

Happiness and a healthy self-esteem will lift your spirits. It will improve your relationship with yourself and with other people. It will prove to you that you are a divine being and you deserve love, happiness, peace, and joy in your life. You are worthy of having all your dreams become your reality if they are for your highest good.

In what areas do you find yourself competing? Why are you competing? What can you do to release that competition? What can you do to focus on the strengths you have to offer the world and what strengths others have to offer? The reason people have different strengths is to help each other, not to compete against one another or to compete against ourselves.

When you are feeling competitive, affirm to yourself: *I am perfect as I am now. Others are perfect as they are right now. I am grateful for the talents I bring to the world. I am grateful to reap the benefits of other people's talents. Knowing that we are all one, I want the best for me and others. There is enough for everyone.*

Compliment Others

Compliment three people today. Choose three men, three women, three children, the first three people you meet, three strangers or three friends. Chances are the three people you'll compliment today are the three that could use a friendly acknowledgement on your part. Be honest and sincere. Choose compliments that are based on personal qualities rather than external factors. Opt for recognizing someone's creativity rather than a beautiful sweater. Notice someone's great disposition rather than a sports car.

Listen to how people respond to you. Do they smile and say thank you or do they downplay the compliment? If people reject your compliments, don't allow it. Be genuine and insisting. Let them know how much you respect that quality in them. At the end of the day, write down the compliments you paid, to whom, and what the responses were. Were the compliments easy for you to give? Were the compliments easy for the other person to receive?

Your challenge is to make this three-a-day pattern part of your everyday life. The brightness that you offer people with a compliment can make a positive difference in their lives. And they, in turn, will affect people in a more positive way. Imagine the wonderful snowball effect that can take place from a simple compliment! Imagine how the self-esteem of your community can grow!

Stepping Out

The Universe makes no mistakes. It is no mistake that we are here on this earth. It is no mistake that we are here to live in joy, to be at peace, to learn, to create and to evolve.

The mistake that occurs is in not stepping out into a new reality based in love, courage and power. Instead we choose to retreat to our familiar, fear-based reality, where we are complacent, addicted to misery, afraid of happiness, forward-thinking, stuck in the past and envious of others. We act like martyrs, think negatively and delay our gratification.

The ultimate truth is that we create our reality through our conscious and subconscious thoughts. There are times when many of us live in blame, fear and doubt, uncertain how to change our realities and our lives. What we are doing as a society is avoiding our internal discomfort, unhappiness, dissatisfaction and procrastination and attempting to replace it with external comforts. We buy expensive wardrobes, cars and houses. We move at a rapid pace, multi-tasking and choosing to be continually distracted in our lives with cell phones, music and television. We over consume food, alcohol, drugs and material possessions.

How can we alter our current reality? How can we move the focal point of our lives from external physical comfort to internal mental peace? And once we find that internal peace, how can we maintain it?

The biggest step we can take is to slow down and get conscious. Turn off your electronic gadgets and check in with yourself. Breathe. Relax. Let go of your stress. Clear your mind. Release your tension. Take time throughout your day to be with yourself. Take time to transition between activities. Meditate. Take time to enjoy who *you* are and what *you* love. And as you begin to learn what you love, *learn to love yourself.* Get to know your truest self and your deepest desires. You create your reality. If your life is too busy, you are the only one who can slow it down. Eliminate unnecessary activities. Stop creating distractions.

As you begin to slow down your life and minimize distractions, you will discover what it is you really want to create in your life and in your world.

This book has brought to light the nine scoundrels that can keep you from living a life of joy. With the explanation of each scoundrel came questions and suggestions for releasing that scoundrel from your life. Here is yet another opportunity to clear away old patterns and move forward into a life of joy. Ask yourself the following questions:

What is the primary purpose of my life right now? What is my mission?
What do I love to do? What brings me joy?
Which scoundrel, or pattern, do I continue to entertain in my life?
What do I need to do to release that scoundrel and have a life of continual joy? What is one specific way I can do this right now?

Before you finish reading the rest of this section, answer those seven questions. Get a pen and paper. Write down your most sincere answers. You will gain very little from the next several paragraphs if your only goal is to finish reading this book. Reading is a passive activity. You are not stepping out into the world when you are passive. If you really want to step out, stop reading and start writing.

Pay particular attention to your last answer. What can you do *right now* to live a life of ultimate joy?

Can you do it? How will you do it?

This may be the point where your fear will erupt and your inner critic will tell you how ridiculous you and your ideas are. This is the point that you tell your fear and your critic to shut up. Shed all fear and all doubt right now. Neither is conducive to a life of joy. They do not serve you in any manner. Throw your fear to the curb and take action. Make a commitment here and now to yourself and to the Universe that you will be consistent in that one action that will free you from the pattern that has kept you from joy and that will now open the channel to a life of joy.

Unearth the purpose of your life. Live with that purpose in your mind's eye with every thought, word and action. Follow your heart. Live with passion.

If you truly want to step out, make today your day to move toward your ideal reality. Make your move toward continual internal peace. Stop complaining. Stop waiting. Stop talking yourself out of your dreams.

Step out into the world.

Move slowly and deliberately. Get CONSCIOUS. Notice signs. Follow your intuition. But do not procrastinate. It's time to step out and begin a new journey in life.